THE SOY
ALTERNATIVE

THE SOY
ALTERNATIVE

whitecap

CONTENTS

THE SOY STORY

There is an ever-increasing tide of information about the many health and nutritional benefits of soy foods, matched by a steady stream of soy-based products appearing on supermarket shelves. This book aims to help you incorporate more soy into your diet with a selection of delicious recipes ranging from breakfast to dessert. Both vegetarians and meat eaters will find a wealth of ideas to suit their eating habits.

The more we find out about the humble soy bean, the better the news seems to get. This book does not eliminate any particular foods such as eggs or dairy products, but rather uses soy foods in conjunction with more traditional ingredients to help you enjoy the benefits of this versatile bean and its many products without radically changing your diet.

THE ADAPTABLE BEAN

The soy bean has many offshoots: it is boiled, puréed, diluted, sweetened and strained to make soy milk; liquefied with water, coagulated, and set to make tofu; fermented to make tempeh; processed into dried bean curd wrappers; sprouted to make soy bean sprouts; salted and fermented to make miso and a variety of sweet and savoury bean pastes; roasted and ground to make a high-protein flour; the oil is extracted for cooking... And that's not all. Products such as soy-based cheese, cream cheese, yoghurt, ice cream, puff pastry and chocolate are creeping onto supermarket shelves. Often these products are not entirely integrated into the mainstream shelving system and can be found in the natural or health food sections.

HEALTH BENEFITS OF SOY

Soy beans contain more protein than any other legume so most soy products are an excellent source of non-animal protein. They are also a good source of soluble fibre (which helps reduce the risk of digestive disorders), omega-3 fatty acids (essential to the proper functioning of the central nervous system), iron, B vitamins, vitamin E, potassium, zinc and other essential minerals. Soy has an indirect impact on calcium levels by enhancing calcium retention. While animal protein has been shown to increase calcium excretion, soy protein does not result in an increased loss of calcium in urine. The ability to retain calcium is particularly important for maintaining healthy bones.

Soy foods are generally dairy-free (check the labels as some products such as soy cheese can contain dairy proteins) and can therefore be enjoyed by people who are lactose intolerant. They can be useful in easing the symptoms of menopause as they contain phytoestrogens which are believed to help alleviate the effects of low oestrogen production in the body. And, soy products can be useful in the dietary treatment of diabetes as soy beans have a low glycaemic index and are cholesterol-free.

It took a long time for soy beans to gain acceptance in the West, purely because they were seen as being conventional beans and, therefore, cooked in the same way. But, soy beans are an extremely tough bean and even after hours of boiling, still have a bitter flavour. Eaten whole, they are indigestible—meaning the valuable protein content becomes useless as it passes straight through the body's system. In eastern countries, soy beans are not eaten in their natural state, but are processed into very different products (soy sauce, tofu, tempeh, miso paste) in order to make the protein digestible. Soy sauce was the first of these products. It was brought to the West by traders in the 1600s and became a popular condiment.

WHERE THE BEAN BEGAN

So where did this wonder bean come from? The soy bean plant is native to China and has been used extensively in Chinese cuisine since the beginning of recorded history more than 4,000 years ago. The small, bushy soy bean plant bears clusters of hairy seed pods attached directly to the stem, each containing two to three seeds which may be green, yellow or black. The soy bean first arrived in Europe in 1692 when a German botanist returned from a visit to Japan. Later, in 1854, an American expedition to Japan brought back two varieties, but it was quite some time before the bean was embraced. It was not until the 20th century that scientific research revealed its great nutritional qualities. There are over a thousand varieties of soy beans, but very few are marketed commercially. There are two main varieties of soy beans grown in Western countries—one for commercial use and the other for eating fresh or dried.

SELECTING SOY PRODUCTS

Be aware that soy products vary in quality and characteristics from brand to brand. Soy milks can vary greatly in consistency and contents, for instance: some soy milks are sweeter and creamier than others and can be purchased malt-free, calcium-enriched, fresh or in long-life cartons, as well as in different flavours. The recipes in this book will specify if a particular soy milk is required, such as creamy or flavoured.

The three types of tofu used in this book are silken, silken firm and firm. Each is different in texture and responds differently to particular cooking methods. Every tofu recipe in this book will specify which type to use to achieve the best results. The texture and flavour of tofu also varies from brand to brand.

There is an important distinction between soy spread or margarine and soy butter. In the recipes in this book, they are NOT interchangeable. Soy butter does not respond well to melting, but is suitable for rubbing into flour for pastries and crumble toppings. It is best to use soy margarine for melting.

Since agriculture first began, man has been trying to produce more food by altering the plants he grows. Farmers discovered they could improve their crops by cross-pollinating the most desirable characteristics from other plants. This traditional process of cross breeding has certain natural limitations, but ensures that evolution occurs at a reasonable pace. Recently, scientists have been able to use genetic engineering to modify the make up of plants and animals, and can now identify a 'desirable' gene within an organism and transplant it elsewhere. Genetic engineering is a very important issue, because it could affect other plants, human health, animals, food production and the environment as a whole for the rest of human history.

DOES GENETIC MODIFICATION AFFECT SOY FOODS?

Genetic modification (GM) refers to the process of introducing, deleting or enhancing particular characteristics depending on whether they are desirable or undesirable. GM foods are produced from plants, animals, or micro-organisms that have been genetically altered or contain ingredients produced by genetically altered organisms (eg. soy milk, wine, cheese and other processed foods).

There is much discussion about GM foods, including soy beans and its products. Many people are concerned about the effects of GM foods on human health and the environment. Others argue it can make food production and transportation more cost efficient, resulting in cheaper foods for the consumer. Listed below are some of the pros and cons of genetic modification.

THE POTENTIAL BENEFITS OF GM

✓ Could produce tastier, cheaper, healthier foods, requiring less processing, have a longer storage time or retain more taste and texture after freezing.
✓ Crops can grow in harsh environments, produce greater yields, or resist pests and diseases, resulting in less wastage, more economical production and ultimately lower food costs.
✓ Crops resistant to pests or disease could reduce the use of chemical sprays.

THE POTENTIAL PROBLEMS OF GM

✗ Disrupts the natural order of genes within the host DNA and brings about combinations of genes that wouldn't occur naturally.
✗ Using genes from animals in plant foods poses ethical and religious problems for many people.
✗ GM crops with in-built pesticides would increase the number of pests resistant to these chemicals. There is a danger that genes coded to resist chemical herbicides could be transferred from GM plants to weeds by pollination, producing tougher weeds.
✗ Antibiotic resistant genes are often used as a marker to test if the plant has taken the new gene. If these genes were copied from the GM plant by a bacteria that causes human disease, that disease could no longer be treated with that antiobiotic.

GLOSSARY
OF INGREDIENTS

If you thought the only soy-based product around was tofu, then you will be pleasantly surprised by the amazing range of products and ingredients made from soy beans. They are becoming more popular and, therefore, more accessible. But not all the entries in this glossary are soy-based—there are other 'unusual' ingredients used in the following recipes. Generally, they should all be available in supermarkets, health food stores or specialist shops.

BEAN CURD SHEETS

Fried bean curd skin is available seasoned or unseasoned. Available pre-split to use as pouches for inari sushi, or unsplit to be sliced in soups and other dishes. Available in Asian grocery stores.

BLACK BEANS

A black soy bean, available dried, fermented, salted and canned in brine. Do not confuse these beans with turtle beans (sometimes labelled as black beans) which are used in South American cooking.

CHILLI BEAN PASTE

Is made from fermented soy beans and is often labelled as chilli bean sauce despite its thick consistency. Chilli bean sauce should be used sparingly and has a long shelf life.

GLUTEN FLOUR

Gluten is a wheat protein that gives structure to yeast-raised breads. It can be added to soy flour (which has no gluten) to improve the texture of baked foods.

GROUND BEAN SAUCE (TIM MEIN JEUNG)

Is made from fermented soy beans which are then ground into a smooth paste. It has a sweet and salty flavour, and a long shelf life.

LECITHIN MEAL

Is a mixture of lecithin, raw wheat germ and wholemeal flour. Lecithin is a nutrient extracted from soy beans that plays a beneficial role in fat and cholesterol metabolism.

LSA MIX

Is a combination of linseed, sunflower seeds and almonds. LSA mix is available ground and in seed form—ground LSA mix should be stored in a sealed container in the refrigerator. Available from health food stores.

MISO

A protein-rich paste made from fermented soy beans and grains. Yellow and white miso pastes have a mild flavour, while red and brown pastes are saltier and more pungent.

SOY BEANS (CANNED)

These soy beans are pre-cooked and packed in brine, and should be rinsed well before using. Soy beans provide the best quality protein of all pulses.

SOY BEANS (DRIED)

Small, oval, yellow beans that require soaking before cooking. They require a longer cooking time than most other beans—usually around 2 hours, depending on the size of the bean.

SOY BEANS (FRESH)

The fresh beans or whole, young pods are available frozen from Asian grocery stores. Depending on seasonal conditions, they are sometimes available in their fresh form.

SOY BEAN SPROUTS

Soy beans can be sprouted and used in the same way as other bean sprouts. They can grow up to twice the size of mung bean sprouts, with a stronger flavour and coarser texture.

SOY BUTTER

Is made of soy bean extract and vegetable oil. It can be used as a spread and for baking purposes, but is not appropriate for melting. It is cholesterol- and lactose-free.

SOY CHEESE

Soy cheeses vary in texture (creamy, soft or firm) and flavour (combined with herbs and spices). Soy cheeses do not contain lactose, therefore do not brown well.

SOY CHOCOLATE

Is a combination of soy extract and cocoa liquor. It is dairy-, lactose- and cholesterol-free—great for those who are lactose intolerant and love their chocolate.

SOY FLOUR

Is made from roasted soy beans that
have been ground into a fine powder.
It is rich in protein and is gluten-free.
Because of its short shelf life, store soy
flour in an airtight container in the
refrigerator. (See page 23)

SOY GRITS

Whole soy beans that have been lightly
toasted and cracked into small pieces.
They need to be soaked before using.
Pre-soaked grits will keep in the
refrigerator for 4 days in a sealed
container.

SOY MAYONNAISE

Is made from soy beans, soy bean oil
and then seasoned with vinegar, sugar
and salt—some contain eggs. It is
available in different flavours such as
herb or garlic.

WHAT IS SOY FLOUR?

Soy flour was first produced in the United States, and began being used commercially in various products from the early 1940s. The soy bean produces a creamy and quite distinctively nutty flavoured flour. It is generally used in combination with wheat flours in home baking and is used extensively in food manufacturing to take advantage of its excellent binding properties.

To make soy flour, soy beans are cleaned, cracked and hulled, broken down into chips and then flakes. The oil and soluble carbohydrates are extracted, leaving soy grits. These grits are then ground into flour.

Soy flour contains more protein than any other type of flour, and so is incorporated into many baked products such as bread or muffins to increase the protein content. It is a very good source of magnesium, thiamine and iron. There is a non-fat soy flour available that actually contains more protein, carbohydrates, minerals and dietary fibre than the regular full-fat variety.

It is a product with many benefits for those on a gluten-free diet. However, it is this lack of gluten that makes it unable to be used as a direct substitute for wheat or rye flour. To incorporate soy flour into a recipe you already have, simply replace up to 30 per cent of the required flour with soy flour. That is, if your recipe calls for 100 g flour, use 30 g soy flour together with 70 g of the usual flour. It may be necessary to add a little more liquid to compensate for its absorbency. Soy flour will create quite a stiff dough, while producing a soft crumb.

It may also be used to thicken sauces and gravies, and is also very good in frying batters as it helps to reduce the amount of fat absorbed.

Soy flour is available from health food stores and will keep stored in the refrigerator or freezer for up to 12 months.

SOY MILK

Is available in thin or creamy textures, calcium- or vitamin-fortified, malt-free, fat-reduced and in a variety of flavours. Available fresh or in long-life cartons. Always check the labels as some brands have added sweeteners. (See page 27)

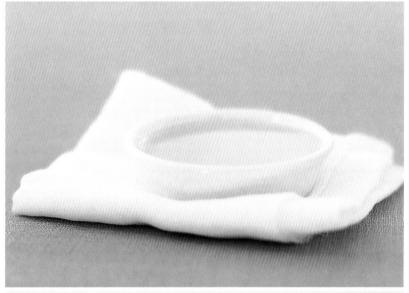

SOY OIL

A natural oil extracted from whole soy beans that can be used as a cooking or salad oil. It is cholesterol-free and contains omega-3 fatty acids—essential for nervous system functioning and reducing the risk of heart disease.

SOY PASTA

Contains soy flour and added soy proteins in addition to the usual durum wheat flour. Available in supermarkets and health food stores.

SOY SPREAD OR MARGARINE

Is made from soy bean oil and is predominantly polyunsaturated. Use as a spread and in cooking. Appropriate when melting is required.

SOY YOGHURT

Is made from soy milk and added cultures. Its consistency varies from brand to brand—some are quite thick while others are runny. It is available in many different flavours or plain.

TEMPEH

Is made by mixing hulled and slightly split soy beans with a vegetarian fermenting agent. The beans are then bound together to form a firm cake. Is available plain or seasoned.

WHAT IS SOY MILK?

Soy milk was developed quite specifically from soy beans to fulfil a need in the market for a dairy milk substitute. It can be used in many of the same ways as dairy milk, and is a convenient substitute for those who are lactose intolerant, or for people who wish to avoid animal products or animal fat. The fat contained in soy milk is unsaturated and, compared with regular full-fat milk, contains no cholesterol and only one third the amount of fat that is present in regular milk. It is a good source of protein, thiamine, iron, phosphorous, copper, potassium and magnesium, and contains very little sodium. Some brands are fortified with calcium, Vitamin D and Vitamin B_{12} which are not naturally found in soy milk.

Soy milk is an easy and convenient way of incorporating soy in your diet. Although it may be used as a substitute for dairy milk in many cases, be aware that there will be discernible differences in flavour. However, particularly in cooking, this is usually masked by the other ingredients present in the dish. Soy milk may tend to darken slightly upon being heated. Other soy dairy substitutes are not so easily interchangeable. For example, soy cream cheese may be used in cooking, but soy sour cream should not be heated. Soy cheese will only melt like dairy cheese if it contains a certain cows milk derivative. Soy butter will not melt, but soy margarine can be used quite effectively instead.

Soy milk is made by soaking soy beans with water, grinding them with more water, bringing to the boil, then filtering off the liquid. The result is soy milk in its purest form, with a distinctive flavour and odour that is generally treated to make it more acceptable for the Western palate.

To make your own soy milk, cover 200 g dried soy beans with water and soak overnight. Drain and rinse, then blend with 2 cups (500 ml) boiling water until very smooth. Pour into a muslin-lined sieve over a large saucepan, and press down to extract as much of the liquid as possible. Place over medium heat and simmer, stirring continuously, until the liquid foams up. Remove from the heat and stand for 1 minute. Place back over low heat and simmer for 10 minutes, stirring continuously to prevent it from sticking. Cool, and add enough water to make up to 2 cups (500 ml) of liquid. Sweeten to taste with sugar or honey. Homemade soy milk will keep refrigerated for up to 3 days.

Be aware that homemade soy milk will not have the same nutritional value as store-bought processed brands, which have usually been fortified with calcium and vitamins.

TOFU DESSERT

A layer of creamy, silken tofu topped with a layer of fruit (several flavours are available) and is usually available in 200 g tubs. Eaten straight from the tub or used as an ingredient in desserts such as bavarois.

TOFU (FIRM)

It holds its shape when cooking and can be sliced, cubed and crumbled—use in stir-fries, pan-fries and baking. Blending is not recommended.

TOFU (FRIED PUFFS)

Are cubes of tofu that have been aerated and deep-fried. They are suitable for use in stir-fries, curries, laksas and soups. They are available from Asian food stores.

TOFU (HARD)

A harder, compressed and salted version of firm tofu. It holds its shape during cooking. Refrigerate leftover tofu in a sealed container filled with water—it will keep up to 5 days if the water is changed every day or two.

TOFU (SILKEN)

Has a smooth, silky texture and, when blended, is similar to cream. It doesn't stir-fry well due to its delicate texture and is often added to soups in cubes, or blended in desserts and smoothies.

TOFU (SILKEN FIRM)

This has the same smooth, custard-like texture as silken tofu only firmer. When blended, the texture is similar to a heavy cream or yoghurt. Can be deep-fried and used in soups.

WHAT IS TOFU?

'Beancurd', usually known by its Japanese name 'tofu', is one of the most significant soy bean by-products due to its exceptional nutritional value. Although soy beans, and most of its products, are very good sources of protein, processing soy into tofu makes it easier for the body to digest. This is particularly important in Asian countries where it is widely consumed—it contains an essential amino acid which is lacking in rice. A serving of 115 g tofu will provide one quarter of your daily protein requirement.

The making of tofu begins with soy beans being soaked in water until soft. They are drained, then ground with fresh water to a purée, strained to produce soy milk, which is then boiled. A coagulant is added, which sets the milk into curds, which is then strained through muslin and pressed to form fresh tofu. The entire process is very similar to cheese making.

The four different types of fresh tofu vary in firmness, texture and nutritional value. Extra firm tofu contains the least amount of water so that it keeps its shape during preparation and cooking. It contains the most protein and has the highest fat content. Firm tofu is not quite as solid, but is still suitable for cooking. It has a very similar fat and protein count to extra firm tofu. Soft tofu contains more liquid making it perfect for use in dressings and sauces. Silken tofu has not been pressed, simply coagulated and the whey drained, hence its fragility and delicate flavour. Of all the tofu, this one contains the least amount of protein, but also the least amount of fat.

It is true that tofu has a rather bland flavour. However, this can be looked at in a positive way—it can be marinated to take on almost any flavour, making it quite flexible in the type of dishes it is used in. The differences in texture means that there is a type suitable for most methods of cooking.

There are some forms of tofu available that have already been cooked. Deep-fried tofu puffs commonly used in laksa, are quite spongy in texture, and are delicious as they absorb the flavour of the dish they are used in. 'Abura-age' are deep-fried thin slices of tofu, used in Japan, filled with sushi rice and vegetables to make inari-zushi. Bean curd skins, 'yuba' are actually a by-product of the tofu making process. A skin forms on the surface of hot soy milk when it stands. This is lifted off and dried. It is used softened to wrap food in, prior to cooking.

Tofu is available at Asian food stores and most supermarkets. Once the packet has been opened, drain off the liquid and store covered with fresh water for 3–4 days in the refrigerator, changing the water every day or two.

SOY FOR BREAKFAST

As kids, we were told that breakfast is the most important meal of the day—a bowl of cereal or toast gave us the energy to run around and play games for hours...until the next meal. We still need that nutritious 'kick-start', but these days we're often too busy to ensure we get it properly. So, instead of just a strong black coffee for your morning pick-up, try a bowl of Bircher Muesli, toasted Banana Bread or fluffy Soy Pancakes to get you up and running.

BIRCHER MUESLI

SERVES 6–8

Originally served with milk, this Swiss-German breakfast dish is named after Dr Bircher-Benner, who served it to his patients at his natural health clinic in Zurich.

Preparation time: 10 minutes +
    overnight soaking
Total cooking time: 8 minutes

1 cup (250 ml) fresh orange juice
2 tablespoons maple syrup
1 teaspoon vanilla essence
100 g silken tofu
1½ cups (150 g) rolled oats
½ cup (60 g) slivered almonds,
    toasted
½ cup (80 g) sultanas
1 cup (250 g) vanilla soy yoghurt
200 g mixed fresh fruit

1 Combine the orange juice, maple syrup, vanilla essence and tofu in a food processor until well combined—the mixture will be slightly grainy. Place the oats in a large bowl. Pour in the tofu mixture and stir together. Cover with plastic wrap and soak overnight in the refrigerator.

2 Preheat the oven to warm 170°C (325°F/Gas 3). Spread the almonds evenly on a baking tray and toast for 5–8 minutes, or until golden.

3 Before serving, stir in the sultanas and toasted almonds to the oat mixture. Serve topped with the vanilla soy yoghurt and mixed fresh fruit.

SWEET BREAKFAST COUSCOUS

SERVES 4–6

If you love couscous, don't restrict yourself to serving it with vegetables. Couscous makes a great base for a fruit-topped breakfast dish that's a little lighter than muesli or porridge.

Preparation time: 10 minutes +
    50 minutes soaking
Total cooking time: 5 minutes

½ cup (90 g) soy grits
1 cup (250 ml) sweetened
    apple juice
¼ cup (40 g) sultanas
¼ cup (45 g) dried apricots,
    cut into strips
1 cinnamon stick
2 tablespoons honey
1⅓ cups (245 g) instant couscous
1 red apple, grated
⅓ cup (40 g) toasted slivered
    almonds
warmed vanilla soy milk, to serve
4 tablespoons soy vanilla yoghurt

1 Soak the soy grits in cold water for 30 minutes. Drain and squeeze dry.

2 Place the apple juice in a saucepan, then add the sultanas, apricots, cinnamon stick and honey and leave to soak for 15 minutes, or until the fruit is plump. Bring the pan to the boil, then turn off the heat. Add the couscous and soy grits, cover with a tea towel and leave for 5 minutes. Remove the cinnamon stick.

3 Run a fork through the couscous to separate the grains, then leave to cool.

4 Stir in the grated apple and toasted almonds. Divide among serving bowls and serve with warmed soy milk and a dollop of soy yoghurt.

BIRCHER MUESLI

BANANA BREAD

SERVES 6

This recipe is a good way of using up overripe bananas sitting in your fruit bowl. However, if your bananas aren't quite ripe enough, place them in a paper bag with a ripe banana or apple to ripen.

Preparation time: 15 minutes + overnight resting
Total cooking time: 1 hour

125 g soy butter
3/4 cup (140 g) soft brown sugar
2 eggs
3/4 cup (90 g) self-raising flour
1/4 cup (20 g) soy flour
1/2 teaspoon bicarbonate of soda
1 teaspoon vanilla essence
3 ripe bananas, mashed (660 g)
1/2 cup (60 g) walnuts, chopped
icing sugar, to dust
fresh fruit, to serve
vanilla soy yoghurt, to serve

1 Preheat the oven to moderate 180°C (350°F/Gas 4). Grease a 10 cm x 20 cm loaf tin and line the base with baking paper.

2 Beat the soy butter and sugar with electric beaters until smooth and creamy. Add the eggs one at a time, beating well after each addition. Sift the self-raising and soy flours with the bicarbonate of soda and add to the egg and butter mixture with the vanilla and banana. Fold the walnuts into the mixture using a metal spoon.

3 Spoon the bread mixture into the prepared tin and bake for 1 hour, or until a skewer comes out clean when inserted into the centre of the bread. Cool slightly, then transfer to a wire rack. When completely cold, wrap in foil and leave overnight.

4 Cut into thick slices and toast to your liking. Dust with icing sugar and serve with fresh fruit and a dollop of vanilla soy yoghurt.

BARLEY WITH CARAMELISED APPLE

SERVES 4

Porridge made with barley is more delicate than oatmeal porridge and is usually made with milk (or soy milk in this case) rather than water.

Preparation time: 15 minutes
Total cooking time: 45 minutes

1.4 litres soy milk
2 cups (440 g) pearl barley
4 apples
50 g soy spread or margarine
1/2 cup (80 g) sultanas
1 teaspoon ground cinnamon
1/4 teaspoon ground nutmeg
pinch ground cloves
1 teaspoon vanilla essence
1/2 cup (95 g) soft brown sugar
1/2 cup (45 g) desiccated coconut
2 tablespoons roasted and chopped
    macadamia nuts

1 Place the soy milk, barley and a pinch salt in a saucepan. Simmer over medium heat, stirring occasionally, for 30 minutes, or until it softens.

2 Peel and cut the apples into 2 cm cubes. Melt the soy spread in a frying pan over medium heat. Add the apple and sauté for 2 minutes. Add the sultanas, cinnamon, nutmeg, ground cloves and vanilla and cook for a further 2 minutes. Add the sugar and cook for 10 minutes, or until the sugar has dissolved and the apple has caramelised.

3 Add the apple mixture to the barley and cook over medium heat for 1 minute, or until warmed through. Serve topped with the coconut and macadamias.

CORN CAKES WITH TOMATO SALSA

SERVES 4

Corn is the only cereal crop native to the Americas, originating in prehistoric Mexico. Along with squash, beans and chillies, it sustained the North American Indians, as well as the Mayans, Incas and Aztecs.

Preparation time: 15 minutes
Total cooking time: 15 minutes

TOMATO SALSA
2 tablespoons diced red onion
2 firm tomatoes, seeded and diced
1/2 Lebanese cucumber, seeded
   and diced
2 tablespoons flat-leaf parsley,
   chopped
1 tablespoon soy bean oil
1 tablespoon white vinegar

4 fresh corn cobs or 425 g can
   corn kernels, drained
2 spring onions, finely chopped
2 eggs, beaten
3/4 cup (60 g) soy flour
1/3 cup (40 g) plain flour
3/4 cup (185 ml) soy milk
3 tablespoons soy bean oil

1 To make the tomato salsa, place the red onion, tomato, cucumber and parsley in a bowl. Season with salt and freshly ground black pepper, then add the soy oil and vinegar and toss together well to coat.

2 If using fresh corn, remove the kernels by cutting down the length of the cob with a sharp knife. Place the kernels in a small bowl with the spring onions and combine.

3 Whisk together the lightly beaten eggs, soy and plain flours and soy milk in a bowl. Add the corn and spring onion mixture and fold through. Season with salt and freshly ground black pepper.

4 Heat the soy oil in a frying pan. Drop 2 tablespoons of the batter per corn cake (12 cakes in total) and allow enough space for spreading—cook in three batches. Cook over medium heat for 2 minutes, or until golden. Turn over and cook for a further 1–2 minutes, or until golden.

5 To serve, stack three corn cakes on individual plates and top with some tomato salsa.

SCRAMBLED TOFU WITH MUSHROOMS

SERVES 4

When crumbled and cooked the firm tofu in this dish looks incredibly like traditional scrambled eggs, but without the eggs, making it suitable for vegans.

Preparation time: 10 minutes
Total cooking time: 15 minutes

40 g soy spread or margarine
200 g button mushrooms, sliced
1 clove garlic, crushed
2 spring onions, chopped
400 g firm tofu, drained and
    crumbled
1 teaspoon tamari
1 tablespoon finely chopped fresh
    parsley
8 thick slices soy and linseed bread,
    toasted

1 Melt 1 tablespoon of the soy spread in a large frying pan. Add the mushrooms and cook over high heat for 5 minutes, or until the mushrooms start to lose their moisture. Add the garlic and cook a further 5 minutes, or until the liquid has evaporated. Remove from the pan.

2 Melt the remaining soy spread in the pan. Add the spring onions and cook for 30 seconds, or until just wilted. Add the crumbled tofu, tamari and mushrooms and cook, stirring gently, for 2 minutes, or until the tofu is heated through. Stir in the parsley and season with black pepper.

3 To serve, spoon the scrambled tofu onto slices of soy buttered soy and linseed toast and serve immediately.

TOFU, CELERIAC AND POTATO ROSTI

MAKES 16

Celeriac is a form of celery—its base is the size of a medium turnip, while the stem itself is the same as wild celery. Celeriac has a milder, sweeter taste than celery and is also suitable to eat raw or cooked.

Preparation time: 10 minutes
Total cooking time: 40 minutes

2 eggs
2 tablespoons plain flour
2 tablespoons soy flour
600 g floury potatoes
    (King Edward, desiree)
350 g celeriac, peeled
100 g firm tofu
2 cloves garlic, crushed
1 tablespoon chopped fresh mixed
    herbs (chives, parsley, thyme)
3 tablespoons vegetable oil
1½ teaspoons butter

1 Whisk the eggs and flours together in a bowl. Season well with salt and freshly ground black pepper.

2 Grate the potatoes with a course grater, then squeeze out any excess moisture. Add to the egg mixture. Grate the celeriac and tofu and stir into the egg mixture with the garlic and herbs.

3 Heat half the oil and half the butter in a heavy-based non-stick frying pan over low—medium heat. When it starts to foam, spoon ¼ cup of the mixture per rösti into the pan pressing down with a metal spatula to form 8 cm rounds. Cook for 5 minutes on each side, or until crisp and golden. (Add the remaining oil and butter as needed.) Keep warm and repeat with the remaining mixture to make 16 rösti in total.

SCRAMBLED TOFU WITH MUSHROOMS

FRENCH TOAST WITH FRIED TOMATOES

FRENCH TOAST WITH FRIED TOMATOES

SERVES 4

It is best to use day-old bread when making French toast as its slight dryness means it will not absorb as much liquid as fresh bread.

Preparation time: 10 minutes
Total cooking time: 30 minutes

4 vine-ripened tomatoes, cut in half
1 teaspoon sugar
1 tablespoon soy bean oil
1½ cups (200 g) grated soy cheese
¼ cup (5 g) lightly packed
    fresh basil
8 slices soy and linseed bread
2 eggs
¼ cup (60 ml) soy milk
25 g soy spread or margarine
fresh basil sprigs, to garnish

1 Preheat the oven to warm 160°C (315°F/Gas 2–3). Sprinkle the tomato halves with sugar, then season. Heat 1 teaspoon of the oil in a frying pan. Fry the tomatoes cut-side down over high heat for 1–2 minutes, or until a crust has developed—wipe the pan clean. Bake on a tray for 10 minutes.

2 Divide the cheese and basil evenly among 4 slices of bread, then top with the remaining bread slices. Pat down well to form a tight sandwich. Beat the eggs and milk together and season well. Dip the sandwiches in until saturated but not soggy. Heat the soy spread and the remaining oil in the pan. Cook the sandwiches over medium heat for 2 minutes each side, or until crisp and golden. Cut in half and serve with the tomatoes.

TOFU AND POTATO OMELETTE

SERVES 4–6

This omelette is packed with protein, fibre and carbohydrates—the perfect way to start the day. This also makes a suitable dish for brunch.

Preparation time: 15 minutes
Total cooking time: 30 minutes

250 g potatoes, diced
⅓ cup (80 ml) olive oil
1 tablespoon soy bean oil
1 large onion, thinly sliced
2 cloves garlic, crushed
300 g silken firm tofu, diced
2 tablespoons chopped
    fresh parsley
5 eggs
1 tablespoon soy sauce
1 tablespoon rice wine vinegar
200 g trimmed soy bean sprouts
100 g sliced and blanched
    snow peas

1 Boil the potato in salted water for 2 minutes, or until tender. Drain and cool. Combine the oils, then heat 2 tablespoons in a 22 cm non-stick frying pan. Add the onion and cook over low heat for 3 minutes, or until soft. Add the garlic and potato and cook for 30 seconds, turning often. Gently stir in the tofu. Turn off the heat and season well. Stir in the parsley.

2 Gently whisk the eggs—do not overbeat. Stir in the tofu mixture. Reheat the pan with 1½ tablespoons of the oil. Pour in the egg mixture, then cook over low heat for 15–20 minutes, occasionally drawing in the edge until there is no liquid left. Invert the omelette onto a plate, tip back into the pan and cook for 2 minutes. Leave for 5 minutes, then cut into wedges.

3 Combine the soy sauce, rice wine vinegar and remaining oil, add the sprouts and snow peas and toss together. Serve with a wedge of omelette and drizzle with a little extra dressing.

SOY PANCAKES WITH RASPBERRIES AND MAPLE SYRUP

SERVES 4-6

Any berries (blackberries, blueberries, strawberries) can be used instead of raspberries—a combination of more than one berry makes another colourful alternative.

Preparation time: 10 minutes + 15 minutes standing
Total cooking time: 20 minutes

1 cup (125 g) plain flour
1/2 cup (60 g) soy flour
1 tablespoon baking powder
2 tablespoons sugar
65 g silken tofu
13/4 cups (425 ml) vanilla soy milk
50 g soy spread or margarine, melted
   and cooled
500 g raspberries
1/2 cup (155 ml) maple syrup
icing sugar, to dust

1 Sift the plain and soy flours, baking powder and 1/2 teaspoon salt together in a large bowl, then stir in the sugar. Place the tofu, soy milk and 1 tablespoon of the melted soy margarine in a food processor and combine until the mixture is smooth. Add to the dry ingredients and mix together well. Cover with plastic wrap and leave for 15 minutes.

2 Heat some of the remaining soy spread in a frying pan over medium heat. Drop 2 tablespoons of the pancake mixture in the pan and cook for 1–2 minutes, or until bubbles form on the surface. Turn and cook the other side for 1 minute, or until golden. Keep warm and repeat with the remaining batter to make 12 pancakes in total.

3 To make the syrup, place the raspberries and maple syrup in a saucepan and stir to coat. Gently cook for 1–2 minutes, or until the berries are warm and well coated in the syrup.

4 Place 2 or 3 pancakes on each plate, serve with the maple raspberries and dust with icing sugar.

SOY BREAKFAST
IN A GLASS

Clockwise from top left:
Strawberry soy lassi, Fresh date and pear shake,
Carob peanut smoothie, Spiced melon shake,
Tropical morning smoothie, and Maple banana breakfast.

SOY BREAKFAST IN A GLASS

Drinks are one of the easiest ways to incorporate soy products into your diet. Blend soy milk, soy yoghurt and silken tofu with your favourite fresh flavouring to produce a delicious and healthy shake.

STRAWBERRY SOY LASSI

Blend 250 g fresh strawberries, 300 g strawberry soy yoghurt, 2 tablespoons honey, 50 ml water and 4 ice cubes in a blender until smooth. Makes two 250 ml glasses.

FRESH DATE AND PEAR SHAKE

Blend 400 ml creamy soy milk, 4 fresh chopped dates and 2 small ripe chopped pears in a blender until smooth. Makes two 350 ml glasses.

CAROB PEANUT SMOOTHIE

Blend 400 ml carob or chocolate soy milk drink, 2 very ripe chopped bananas, 150 g silken tofu, 2 tablespoons honey and 1 tablespoon peanut butter in a blender until smooth. Makes three 250 ml glasses.

SPICED MELON SHAKE

Lightly crush $1/4$ teaspoon cardamom seeds in a mortar and pestle or with the back of a knife. Place in a blender with 350 ml creamy soy milk and blend for 30 seconds. Strain the soy milk and rinse any remaining seeds from the blender. Return the strained milk to the blender, add 250 g chopped rockmelon, 1 tablespoon honey, 2 tablespoons ground almonds and 4 ice cubes and blend until smooth. Makes two 300 ml glasses.

TROPICAL MORNING SMOOTHIE

Blend 2 chopped mangoes (400 g), 350 ml creamy soy milk, 150 ml pineapple juice, $1/4$ cup (15 g) chopped fresh mint and 6 ice cubes in a blender until smooth. Garnish with a sprig of fresh mint. Makes three 300 ml glasses.

MAPLE BANANA BREAKFAST

Blend 350 ml fresh or creamy soy milk, 150 g vanilla soy yoghurt, 2 very ripe chopped bananas, 1 large ripe chopped yellow peach, 2 teaspoons lecithin meal and 2 tablespoons maple syrup in a blender until smooth. Makes two 375 ml glasses.

SOY FOR LUNCH

Lunchtime meals can be enjoyed at home with a crowd, outdoors on your own or romantically with a view. Serve the family batches of Lentil Soup, pack a few Vietnamese Rice Paper Rolls for a quick bite out of the office or an impressive portable Soy Bean Terrine for two. Tabbouleh, Potato Salad and Pear and Walnut Salad are great additions to any picnic, a packed lunch, or as a light and fresh meal on their own.

CARROT AND LEEK TART

SERVES 6–8

The Emperor Nero is reported to have eaten a lot of leeks as he believed they would improve his singing voice—he was nicknamed 'leek-eater' by his people.

Preparation time: 35 minutes +
    40 minutes chilling
Total cooking time: 1 hour 35 minutes

200 g russet (Idaho) potatoes,
    quartered
1 tablespoon soy milk
1 cup (150 g) wholemeal flour
½ cup (60 g) soy flour
150 g soy spread or margarine
2 carrots (450 g), cut into small
    pieces
2 leeks (450 g), trimmed and
    thinly sliced
1 cup (250 ml) vegetable stock
½ teaspoon sugar
1 tablespoon tomato paste
3 eggs
200 g plain soy yoghurt
1 small carrot, extra
1 small leek, extra
1 tablespoon soy spread or
    margarine, extra

1 Cook the potato in a saucepan of salted boiling water for 8–10 minutes, or until tender. Drain well, return to the pan, add the soy milk and season. Mash until smooth.

2 Place the flours in a bowl and rub in 100 g of the soy spread until it resembles fine breadcrumbs. Add the potato and bring together to form a ball. Cool, then wrap in plastic wrap. Refrigerate for at least 30 minutes.

3 Preheat the oven to moderately hot 200°C (400°F/Gas 6). Roll out the dough and line a 23 cm tart tin with a removable base with the pastry. Trim any excess. Chill for 10 minutes. Line the pastry with baking paper and fill with baking beads or uncooked rice. Bake for 15 minutes. Remove the baking paper and beads and bake a further 5 minutes, or until slightly golden. Reduce the oven to moderate 180°C (350°F/Gas 4).

4 Melt the remaining soy spread in a saucepan. Add the carrot, leek and 2 tablespoons water and sauté gently for 10 minutes, or until the liquid has evaporated. Add the stock and sugar and cook for 20 minutes, or until tender and all the liquid has been absorbed. Cool slightly, then add the paste, sugar, eggs and yoghurt. Place in a food processor and blend until smooth. Season. Pour into the pastry case and bake for 20–25 minutes, or until set and lightly golden on top.

5 Peel the extra carrot into thin ribbons with a vegetable peeler. Slice the extra leek lengthways into thin ribbons. Melt the extra soy spread in a frying pan. Add the carrot and leek and saute for 8 minutes, or until softened. Pile in the centre of the tart just before serving.

SOY AND MUSHROOM BURGERS

SERVES 4

Why should a non-meat eater miss out on such a classic portable meal? Here the traditional beef patty is replaced with one made from protein-packed soy beans and mushrooms—'meat for vegetarians'.

Preparation time: 25 minutes
Total cooking time: 15 minutes

2 tablespoons soy bean oil
1 onion, finely chopped
200 g field or cap mushrooms,
    finely chopped
1 clove garlic, crushed
420 g can soy beans, rinsed and
    drained
1½ cups (120 g) fresh wholemeal
    breadcrumbs
2 teaspoons fresh thyme
1 egg, lightly beaten
4 Turkish bread rolls
1 avocado, mashed
60 g mixed lettuce leaves
purchased tomato chutney,
    to serve

1 Heat 2 teaspoons of the oil in a frying pan. Add the onion and cook, stirring occasionally, over medium heat for 3 minutes, or until soft. Add the mushrooms and garlic and cook, stirring, for 2 minutes, or until just soft. Cool slightly.

2 Place the soy beans in a large bowl and roughly mash with a potato masher. Add the mushroom mixture, breadcrumbs, thyme and egg. Season well with salt and freshly ground black pepper and stir until combined. With wet hands, shape the mixture into 4 patties about 10 cm in diameter.

3 Heat the remaining oil in a frying pan. Cook the patties, in batches, for 2–3 minutes each side, or until golden brown—they will be quite fragile, so handle carefully during cooking.

4 To assemble, split the rolls and toast on both sides. Spread the base with avocado, then top with lettuce, a patty, a dollop of chutney and top with the roll 'lid'.

TOFU AND VEGETABLE KOFTAS
WITH YOGHURT DIPPING SAUCE

SERVES 4

Variations of the kofta (meatballs, rissoles, croquettes, dumplings) are popular all over the world—India, Central Asia, the Middle East, the Balkans and North Africa.

Preparation time: 25 minutes
Total cooking time: 20 minutes

YOGHURT DIPPING SAUCE
200 g plain soy yoghurt
1 clove garlic, crushed
2 tablespoons fresh mint, finely
   chopped

250 g firm tofu
1/3 cup (80 ml) olive oil
11/2 cups (185 g) grated pumpkin
3/4 cup (100 g) grated zucchini

1 onion, chopped
4 cloves garlic, crushed
4 small spring onions, finely
   chopped
1/4 cup (7 g) chopped fresh
   coriander leaves
1 tablespoon Madras curry powder
1/2 cup (50 g) grated Parmesan
1 cup (150 g) wholemeal flour
oil, for deep-frying

1 To make the dipping sauce, place the yoghurt, garlic and mint in a small bowl, season to taste with salt and freshly ground black pepper and mix together well. Add a little water, if needed.

2 To make the koftas, blend the tofu in a food processor or blender until finely processed.

3 Heat the oil in a frying pan. Add the pumpkin, zucchini, onion and garlic and cook, stirring occasionally, over medium heat, for 10 minutes, or until the vegetables are tender. Cool.

4 Add the spring onion, coriander, curry powder, Parmesan, tofu, 1/2 cup (75 g) of the flour and 1 tablespoon salt and mix well. Roll a tablespoon of mixture between your hands to form a ball, then repeat with the remaining mixture. Coat the balls in the remaining flour.

5 Fill a deep heavy-based saucepan one third full of oil and heat to 180°C (350°F), or until a cube of bread browns in 15 seconds. Cook the koftas in small batches for 2–3 minutes, or until golden brown. Drain on paper towels. Serve with the dipping sauce.

TABBOULEH WITH SOY GRITS

TABBOULEH WITH SOY GRITS

SERVES 6–8

Soy grits make this tabbouleh just as delicious as the traditional tabbouleh which is made with burghul (cracked wheat).

Preparation time: 20 minutes + soaking
Total cooking time: Nil

150 g bunch fresh flat-leaf parsley
1 cup (180 g) soy grits
2 tablespoons chopped fresh mint
1 small red onion, cut into
    thin wedges
3 ripe tomatoes, chopped
400 g can chickpeas, rinsed and
    drained
3 tablespoons lemon juice
2 tablespoons extra virgin olive oil
Lebanese or pitta bread, to serve

1 Remove all the parsley leaves from the stalks, roughly chop and place in a large serving bowl.

2 Soak the soy grits in 2/3 cup (170 ml) boiling water for 3 minutes, or until all the water has been absorbed. Add to the parsley, along with the mint, onion, tomato and chickpeas. Drizzle with the lemon juice and olive oil. Season well with salt and freshly ground black pepper and toss together.

3 Serve with Lebanese or pitta bread and Soy Bean Hummus (see page 92) as a vegetarian meal, or as an accompaniment to barbecued meat, chicken or fish.

CREAMY SOY BEAN SOUP

SERVES 6–8

Leeks add extra flavour to this soy bean soup. Leeks are closely indentified with the Welsh, because in the 12th century they wore leeks on their hats to distinguish them from their enemies.

Preparation time: 10 minutes +
    overnight soaking
Total cooking time: 1 hour

1½ cups (320 g) dried soy beans
2 tablespoons extra virgin olive oil
3 brown onions, finely chopped
1 leek (white part), finely chopped
3 cloves garlic
2 stalks celery, finely chopped
1 litre chicken stock
50 ml dry sherry
bouquet garni (bay leaf, thyme sprig,
    rosemary sprig)
½ cup (125 ml) cream
2 tablespoons finely chopped fresh
    flat-leaf parsley
extra virgin olive oil, extra, to drizzle

1 Soak the soy beans overnight in a large bowl of cold water. Drain.

2 Heat the oil in a saucepan. Add the onion and leek and cook gently for 2–3 minutes, or until soft—do not brown. Add the garlic and celery and cook for 1 minute. Add the soy beans, stock and sherry to the pan, then add the bouquet garni. Bring to the boil, then simmer, partially covered, for 45 minutes, or until the beans are soft. Remove the herbs. Cool slightly.

3 Place the soup in a blender and process in batches until puréed. Season well with salt and pepper. Return the soup to the saucepan and stir in the cream. Add the parsley and heat gently, without allowing to boil.

4 Divide among deep soup bowls and drizzle with a little extra virgin olive oil. Serve with crusty bread or thick slices of toast.

PARMESAN-CRUSTED TEMPEH

SERVES 4

The tomato sauce in this recipe freezes beautifully and can be used with pasta or spooned over chicken schnitzels for a 'parmagiana'-style meal.

Preparation time: 25 minutes +
   40 minutes refrigeration
Total cooking time: 45 minutes

300 g tempeh
4 tablespoons plain flour
4 tablespoons finely chopped fresh
   flat-leaf parsley
1 cup (80 g) fresh breadcrumbs
½ cup (50 g) freshly grated
   Parmesan
2 eggs, beaten
2–3 tablespoons soy bean oil

TOMATO SAUCE
1 tablespoon soy bean oil
2 tablespoons finely chopped onion
800 g ripe tomatoes, peeled, seeded
   and chopped
1 tablespoon balsamic vinegar
1 teaspoon sugar
2 teaspoons fresh oregano, chopped

1 Cut the tempeh into 8 fingers. Season the flour with salt and freshly ground black pepper. Combine the parsley, breadcrumbs and Parmesan and season. Coat the tempeh in the flour, dip in the egg, then coat in the breadcrumbs. Place on a foil-lined tray and refrigerate for 20 minutes. Dip the crumbed fingers in the egg again, coat with a second layer of breadcrumbs, then refrigerate for a further 20 minutes.

2 To make the sauce, heat the oil in a saucepan. Add the onion and cook for 5–8 minutes, or until just golden. Add the tomato and simmer, stirring frequently, over medium heat for 20 minutes, or until thickened. Add the vinegar, sugar and oregano. Cook for a further 2 minutes. Keep warm.

3 Preheat the oven to very slow 120°C (250°F/Gas 1–2). Heat the oil in a frying pan. Fry the tempeh in batches for 3 minutes on each side, or until browned. Keep warm in the oven between batches. Top with the sauce and serve with a salad.

VEGETABLE PAKORAS WITH SPICED YOGHURT

SERVES 4

These deep-fried battered vegetables are usually eaten as a starter or a snack in India, Pakistan and Afganistan. This dish is also known as bhajis.

Preparation time: 30 minutes + 15 minutes standing
Total cooking time: 20 minutes

SPICED YOGHURT
1 teaspoon cumin seeds
200 g plain soy yoghurt
1 clove garlic, crushed
1/2 cup (25 g) fresh coriander
   leaves, chopped

1/3 cup (35 g) besan (chickpea
   flour)
1/3 cup (40 g) self-raising flour
1/3 cup (45 g) soy flour
1/2 teaspoon ground turmeric
1 teaspoon cayenne pepper

1/2 teaspoon ground coriander
1 small fresh green chilli, seeded
   and finely chopped
oil, for deep-frying
200 g cauliflower, cut into small
   florets
140 g orange sweet potato, cut
   into 5 mm slices
180 g eggplant, cut into 5 mm
   slices
180 g fresh asparagus, cut into
   6 cm lengths

1 To make the spiced yoghurt, heat a small frying pan over medium heat. Add the cumin seeds and fry for 1–2 minutes, or until aromatic—shake the pan frequently to prevent the seeds from burning. Place in a mortar and pestle or spice grinder and roughly grind. Whisk into the soy yoghurt with the garlic. Season to taste with salt and freshly ground black pepper, then stir in the coriander.

2 To make the pakoras, place the besan, self-raising and soy flours, ground turmeric, cayenne pepper, ground coriander, chopped chilli and 1 teaspoon salt in a bowl. Gradually whisk in 1 cup (250 ml) cold water to form a batter. Leave for 15 minutes.

3 Preheat the oven to very slow 120°C (250°F/Gas 1–2).

4 Fill a small saucepan one third full with oil and heat to 170°C (325°F), or until a cube of bread browns in 20 seconds. Dip the vegetables in the batter and deep-fry in small batches, for 1–2 minutes, or until pale gold. Remove with a slotted spoon and drain on paper towels. Keep warm in the oven until all the vegetables are deep-fried.

5 Serve the vegetable pakoras hot with the spiced yoghurt and a salad.

VIETNAMESE RICE PAPER ROLLS WITH DIPPING SAUCE

MAKES 16

These rice paper rolls are like a fresh version of spring rolls—everyone's favourite Asian entrée—and they'll stay fresh stored in a lunch box until lunchtime.

Preparation time: 40 minutes + 5 minutes soaking
Total cooking time: 2 minutes

50 g dried rice vermicelli
16 square (15 cm) rice paper
    wrappers
1 zucchini, julienned
1 Lebanese cucumber, julienned
1 carrot, grated
200 g frozen soy beans
1 cup (20 g) fresh mint, julienned
100 g tofu, cut into 1 cm wide
    batons

DIPPING SAUCE
1/3 cup (80 ml) fish sauce
2 tablespoons chopped fresh
    coriander leaves
2 small fresh red chillies, finely
    chopped
2 teaspoons soft brown sugar
2 teaspoons lime juice

1 Soak the vermicelli in hot water for 5 minutes, or until soft. Drain and cut into 5 cm lengths with a pair of scissors. Bring a saucepan of water to the boil, add the soy beans and cook for 2 minutes. Drain well.

2 Working with no more than two rice paper wrappers at a time, dip each wrapper in a bowl of warm water for 10 seconds to soften. Drain, then lay out on a flat work surface.

3 Place a small amount of rice vermicelli on the bottom third of a wrapper, leaving a 2 cm border either side. Top with a little zucchini, cucumber, carrot, soy beans, mint and 2 batons of tofu. Keeping the filling compact and neat, fold in both sides and roll up tightly. Seal with a little water, if necessary. Cover with a damp cloth and repeat with the remaining rice paper wrappers and filling ingredients.

4 To make the dipping sauce, place the fish sauce, coriander leaves, chilli, brown sugar, lime juice and 2 tablespoons water in a small bowl and stir together well. Serve with the rice paper rolls.

CHINESE HOT AND SOUR SOUP

Enjoy the delicious tang of opposing flavours in this traditional-style soup. A nice light, yet satisfying, soup suitable as an entrée or main course.

Preparation time: 15 minutes +
    30 minutes soaking
Total cooking time: 15 minutes

8 dried shiitake mushrooms
2 teaspoons cornflour
2 teaspoons sesame oil
1 litre vegetable stock
125 g bamboo shoots, julienned
125 g silken firm tofu, cut into
    7.5 cm long thin strips
2 teaspoons light soy sauce
3 tablespoons white wine vinegar
1/2 teaspoon white pepper
spring onions, thinly sliced, to garnish

1 Soak the mushrooms in 1/2 cup (125 ml) hot water for 30 minutes. Drain and reserve the liquid in a small bowl. Discard the stems and cut the caps into quarters.

2 Whisk the cornflour, sesame oil and 2 tablespoons of the stock together in a small bowl.

3 Place the remaining stock and reserved mushroom liquid in a large saucepan and bring to the boil. Add the mushrooms and bamboo shoots, and season to taste with salt. Reduce the heat and simmer, uncovered, for 5 minutes.

4 Add the tofu, soy sauce, white wine vinegar and white pepper. Return the soup to a simmer. Stir in the cornflour mixture and cook until the soup thickens slightly. Pour into individual serving bowls and garnish with the spring onion.

SOY LENTIL BURGERS WITH PEANUT SAUCE

SERVES 6

Peanuts are commonly mistaken for being a nut, but they're actually a legume. This could explain why they are often called 'Chinese beans' throughout Malaysia and Indonesia.

Preparation time: 20 minutes +
    1 hour refrigeration
Total cooking time: 40 minutes

3 tablespoons soy bean oil
1 large brown onion, finely chopped
1 clove garlic, crushed
1 large carrot, finely grated
2 teaspoons mild curry powder
1 cup (250 g) red lentils, washed
2 cups (500 ml) vegetable stock
250 g firm tofu, drained
1/2 cup (15 g) fresh coriander
    leaves
2 cups (160 g) fresh wholemeal
    breadcrumbs
hamburger buns, to serve
lettuce leaves, to serve

PEANUT SAUCE
3 tablespoons smooth peanut
    butter
2 cloves garlic, crushed
1 tablespoon sesame oil
1 tablespoon soy sauce
1 tablespoon sweet chilli sauce
1/2 cup (125 ml) coconut milk

1 Heat 1 tablespoon of the oil in a frying pan. Add the onion and cook over medium heat for 2–3 minutes, or until lightly golden. Add the garlic, carrot and curry powder and cook for a further 1 minute. Add the lentils and vegetable stock. Cook, stirring occasionally, over low heat for 20 minutes, or until the lentils are cooked. Drain well, then allow to cool slightly.

2 Place half the lentil mixture in a food processor. Add the tofu and coriander leaves and process to combine. Transfer to a bowl, add the breadcrumbs and the remaining lentils and mix together to form a thick mixture. Form into 6 large patties, then cover and refrigerate for 1 hour.

3 Heat the remaining oil in a frying pan. Cook the patties in batches, for 3–4 minutes, or until crispy and golden. Turn over and cook the other side for another 3–4 minutes, or until crispy and golden.

4 To make the peanut sauce, place the peanut butter, garlic, sesame oil, soy and sweet chilli sauces and coconut milk in a bowl. Stir the mixture together until it forms a smooth consistency—add a little water if it is too thick for your liking.

5 Serve the patties on toasted hamburger buns with lettuce greens and the peanut sauce.

PEAR AND WALNUT SALAD WITH LIME VINAIGRETTE

SERVES 4

This dish is similar to the famous Waldorf salad with its fresh combination of fruit and walnuts tossed in a light dressing.

Preparation time: 25 minutes
Total cooking time: 20 minutes

1 small baguette, cut into 16 thin
    slices
soy bean oil, for brushing
1 clove garlic, cut in half
1 cup (100 g) walnuts
200 g soy cheese
400 g mesclun leaves
2 pears, cut into 2 cm cubes, mixed
    with 2 tablespoons lime juice

LIME VINAIGRETTE
3 tablespoons soy bean oil
2 tablespoons lime juice, extra
1/4 cup (60 ml) raspberry vinegar

1 Preheat the oven to moderate 180°C (350°F/Gas 4). Brush the baguette slices with a little oil, rub with the cut side of the garlic, then place on a baking tray. Bake for 10 minutes, or until crisp and golden. Place the walnuts on a baking tray and roast for 5–8 minutes, or until slightly browned—shake the tray to ensure even colouring. Allow to cool for 5 minutes.

2 To make the lime vinaigrette, whisk together the oil, lime juice, raspberry vinegar, 1 teaspoon salt and 1/2 teaspoon freshly ground black pepper in a small bowl. Set aside until ready to use.

3 Spread some of the soy cheese on each crouton, then cook under a hot grill for 2–3 minutes, or until hot.

4 Place the mesclun, pears and walnuts in a bowl, add the vinaigrette and toss through. Divide the salad among four serving bowls and serve with the soy cheese croutons.

SOY BEAN TERRINE

SERVES 6–8

Terrines are easy to transport from the kitchen to the picnic blanket. Sliced and served cold, there is no need to reheat them to enjoy.

Preparation time: 20 minutes +
   overnight soaking
Total cooking time: 2 hours 20 minutes

1 cup (200 g) dried soy beans
1 tablespoon soy bean oil
1 onion, finely chopped
1 zucchini, grated
1/4 cup (7 g) finely chopped fresh
   flat-leaf parsley
1 teaspoon cayenne pepper
3 eggs, lightly beaten
1/3 cup (90 g) sour cream
1/4 cup (60 ml) lemon juice
2 cups (250 g) grated Cheddar
1/2 cup (50 g) grated fresh Parmesan
purchased tomato relish, to serve

1 Place the soy beans in a bowl, pour in plenty of cold water and soak for at least 8 hours, or preferably overnight. Drain well. Place the soy beans in a large saucepan and add enough water to cover the beans. Bring to the boil, then simmer for 1 hour 30 minutes, or until tender.

2 Preheat the oven to moderately hot 190°C (375°F/Gas 5). Lightly grease a 22 x 12 cm loaf tin and line the base and sides with baking paper. Blend the beans in a food processor until crumbly.

3 Heat the oil in a large frying pan. Add the onion and zucchini. Cook over medium heat for 5 minutes, or until golden. Transfer to a bowl and allow to cool.

4 Add the parsley, cayenne pepper, eggs, sour cream, lemon juice, cheeses and soy beans and mix together. Spoon the mixture into the prepared tin and press down to flatten the top. Bake for 45 minutes, or until firm. Cool completely in the tin. Carefully invert on a platter and slice. Serve with the tomato relish and, if desired, a side salad.

POTATO SALAD WITH CREAMY TOFU MAYONNAISE

POTATO SALAD WITH CREAMY TOFU MAYONNAISE

SERVES 4 (AS AN ACCOMPANIMENT)

The pink fir apple is a waxy, slightly elongated potato with pinkish yellow flesh and a nutty flavour. Waxy potatoes are high in moisture and low in starch so they hold their shape when boiled—ideal for salads.

Preparation time: 20 minutes
Total cooking time: 15 minutes

1 kg waxy potatoes (pink fir apple)
300 g silken tofu
2 tablespoons fresh lemon juice
2 teaspoons honey
1 tablespoon light soy sauce
2 teaspoons Dijon mustard
3 tablespoons chopped fresh dill
90 ml olive oil
sprigs of fresh dill, to garnish

1 Scrub the potatoes clean and leave unpeeled. Place in a large saucepan of salted water and bring to the boil. Simmer for 15 minutes, or until tender. Drain well and cool slightly. Cut into 2 cm chunks and place in a bowl.

2 Place the tofu, lemon juice, honey, soy sauce, mustard and dill in a food processor and blend until smooth. Gradually pour in the oil while the machine is still running. Season. Pour the mayonnaise over the potato and mix gently until well coated. Serve warm or cold, garnished with the dill.

POTATO SALAD WITH MISO DRESSING

SERVES 4 (AS AN ACCOMPANIMENT)

Silken tofu has a very silky texture and, when blended, is similar to cream. Combined with the other dressing ingredients, it produces a smooth mayonnaise-like dressing.

Preparation time: 10 minutes + cooling
Total cooking time: 25 minutes

1 kg small chat potatoes or
    1 kg sweet potatoes, peeled,
    and cut into 2 cm cubes
150 g silken tofu
2 tablespoons white miso paste
1 clove garlic
2 tablespoons soy milk
1 tablespoon seasoned rice vinegar
1/2 teaspoon sesame oil
2 spring onions, finely sliced
1 tablespoon toasted sesame seeds
chopped fresh chives, to garnish

1 Place the potatoes in a saucepan of cold water, bring to the boil and cook for 20–25 minutes, or until just tender. Drain, then refresh under cold water. Allow to cool.

2 Blend the tofu, miso paste, garlic, soy milk, rice vinegar and sesame oil in a food processor until smooth. Pour over the potatoes, add the spring onion, then gently toss together until combined.

3 Transfer the potatoes to a serving dish. Sprinkle the sesame seeds over the top and garnish with the chives.

SPICED SOY BEAN PATTIES
WITH SALSA

SERVES 4

Soy bean patties are a versatile filler, either served on their own or with bread, and the tomato and cucumber salsa is a refreshing topping with a contrasting crunchy texture.

Preparation time: 20 minutes
Total cooking time: 15 minutes

SALSA
1 tomato, seeded and diced
1 cucumber, seeded and diced
1/4 red onion, finely chopped
1 tablespoon chopped fresh
    coriander leaves
1 tablespoon chopped fresh mint
2 tablepsoons olive oil
1 tablespoon white wine vinegar

1/2 teaspoon finely grated
    lemon rind
1 tablespoon lemon juice
2 x 300 g cans soy beans, rinsed
    and drained
1/3 cup (10 g) roughly chopped
    fresh flat-leaf parsley
3/4 cup (60 g) fresh breadcrumbs
2 teaspoons ground cumin
2 teaspoons ground coriander
3/4 teaspoon paprika
2 tablespoons soy bean oil
4 slices crusty bread, toasted

1 To make the salsa, place the tomato, cucumber, onion, coriander leaves, mint, olive oil and vinegar in a small bowl and stir together well. Season with salt and freshly ground black pepper.

2 Blend the lemon rind, lemon juice, soy beans and parsley in a food processor in bursts until roughly mashed. Transfer to a bowl and add the breadcrumbs, ground cumin, ground coriander and paprika and mix together well. Divide the mixture into four portions using damp hands. Shape into patties 8 cm in diameter.

3 Heat the oil in a large frying pan over medium heat, add the patties and cook for 3 minutes each side, or until golden brown and cooked through.

4 Serve the patties with crusty bread topped with salsa.

GRILLED TOFU SALAD WITH
GINGER MISO DRESSING

SERVES 4

Miso is a Japanese bean paste (made from soy beans and rice) and plays an important part in their cuisine. It is commonly used on grilled foods, in soups and dressings and as a flavouring for pickles.

Preparation time: 20 minutes +
    overnight marinating
Total cooking time: 5 minutes

1/3 cup (80 ml) tamari, shoyu or
    light soy sauce
2 teaspoons soy bean oil
2 cloves garlic, crushed
1 teaspoon grated fresh ginger
1 teaspoon chilli paste
500 g firm tofu, cut into 2 cm cubes
400 g mesclun leaves
1 Lebanese cucumber, finely sliced
250 g cherry tomatoes, halved
2 teaspoons soy bean oil, extra

DRESSING
2 teaspoons white miso paste
2 tablespoons mirin
1 teaspoon toasted sesame oil
1 teaspoon grated fresh ginger
1 teaspoon finely chopped chives
1 tablespoon toasted sesame seeds

1 Mix the tamari, soy bean oil, garlic, ginger, chilli paste and 1/2 teaspoon salt together well in a bowl. Add the tofu and mix until well coated. Marinate for at least 10 minutes, or preferably overnight. Drain and reserve the marinade.

2 To make the dressing, combine the miso with 1/2 cup (125 ml) hot water until the miso has dissolved. Add the mirin, sesame oil, ginger, chives and sesame seeds and stir thoroughly until it begins to thicken.

3 Combine the mesclun leaves, cucumber and tomatoes in a serving bowl.

4 Heat the extra soy bean oil on a chargrill or hotplate. Add the tofu and cook over medium heat for 4 minutes, or until golden brown. Pour on the reserved marinade and cook a further 1 minute over high heat. Remove from the grill and allow to cool for 5 minutes.

5 Add the tofu to the salad, drizzle with the dressing and toss well. Serve immediately.

LENTIL SOUP WITH SPICED YOGHURT

SERVES 4–6

This delicious soup can have a slightly curdled appearance due to the yoghurt, but this in no way detracts from the flavour of the dish.

Preparation time: 10 minutes
Total cooking time: 25 minutes

1 tablespoon soy bean oil
1 large onion, finely chopped
2 cloves garlic, crushed
1 teaspoon ground cumin
1/2 teaspoon garam masala
1/2 teaspoon sambal oelek
1/4 cup (60 g) tomato paste
1 cup (250 g) red lentils
1 teaspoon sugar
415 g can crushed tomatoes
3 cups (750 ml) vegetable stock
1/2 cup (125 g) plain soy yoghurt
2 tablespoons fresh coriander
  leaves
fresh coriander sprigs, to garnish

SPICED YOGHURT
1 cup (250 g) plain soy yoghurt
2 tablespoons chopped fresh
  coriander leaves
1/2 teaspoon ground coriander
1/2 teaspoon ground cumin
1/2 teaspoon mild paprika

1 Heat the oil in a saucepan. Add the onion and cook over medium heat for 1 minute. Stir in the garlic, cumin, garam masala and sambal oelek and cook for a further 30 seconds, or until fragrant. Add the tomato paste, lentils, sugar, crushed tomatoes, stock and 1 cup (250 ml) water to the saucepan and cook for 20 minutes, or until the lentils are tender.

2 Remove half the soup and leave to cool slightly. Place the cooled portion in a blender, add the yoghurt and coriander leaves and blend together until smooth. Add the blended mixture to the remaining soup and stir well to combine. Keep warm over low heat—do not reboil.

3 To make the spiced yoghurt, combine the yoghurt, fresh and ground coriander, cumin and paprika in a bowl, just before serving.

4 Serve the soup with a dollop of spiced yoghurt, and garnish with a sprig of coriander.

SOY FOR SUNDAY LUNCH

Clockwise from top left:
Five-spice soy chicken,
Pumpkin with miso glaze,
Cauliflower cheese, Potato
and coriander mash, and
Soy beans with spring onions
and snow peas

SOY FOR SUNDAY LUNCH

A good soy baked lunch doesn't mean skimping on your favourites.
With the subtle addition of soy in every dish, you can still enjoy
a mouth-watering roast chicken with mashed potato and vegetables.

FIVE-SPICE SOY CHICKEN

Combine 1/4 cup (60 ml) Japanese soy sauce, 1/4 cup (60 ml) Chinese rice wine, 2 cloves crushed garlic, 1 tablespoon finely chopped fresh ginger, 1/4 cup (90 g) honey, 1/2 teaspoon five-spice powder, 2 tablespoons soy bean oil and 2 teaspoons hot bean sauce in a large ceramic dish. Place a 2 kg chicken in the dish and turn to coat. Spoon some marinade into the cavity. Cover and refrigerate overnight. Preheat the oven to moderately hot 200°C (400°F/Gas 6). Drain and reserve the marinade. Place the chicken on a rack in a roasting tin and pour 2 cups (500 ml) water in the base of the tin. Roast for 1 hour, basting regularly with the reserved marinade (cover with foil if it overbrowns). Maintain the water level in the base of the tin. Cover loosely with foil and rest for 15 minutes before carving. To make the gravy, melt 1 tablespoon soy spread in a small saucepan, stir in 3 tablespoons soy flour and cook for 1 minute. Whisk in the juices from the roasting tin and the reserved marinade, then simmer for 10 minutes, or until smooth and thickened slightly.

POTATO AND CORIANDER MASH

Boil 750 g chopped desiree potatoes with 4 cloves garlic for 20 minutes, or until tender. Drain. Return to the pan with 250 g drained crumbled silken tofu, 2 tablespoons soy spread and 1/3 cup (90 g) soy mayonnaise—mash until smooth and creamy. Stir in 1/4 cup (15 g) finely chopped fresh coriander leaves. Season with salt and pepper.

PUMPKIN WITH MISO GLAZE

Peel and seed 1 butternut pumpkin (600 g) and cut into 6 flat even pieces. Boil for 12 minutes, or until tender. Drain and cool. Preheat the oven to hot 220°C (425°F/Gas 7) and place the pumpkin on a greased baking tray. Combine 2 tablespoons white miso, 1 tablespoon mirin, 1 tablespoon sake, 1 tablespoon lemon juice and 1 teaspoon soft brown sugar. Spread evenly on one flat side of the pumpkin, then sprinkle with 2 teaspoons sesame seeds. Bake for 15 minutes, or until the pumpkin is cooked through. Garnish with finely sliced spring onion.

SOY BEANS WITH SPRING ONIONS AND SNOW PEAS

Trim 525 g bulb spring onions leaving 1 cm of green. Peel off the outer layer and trim the root ends, leaving them intact. Boil for 1 minute. Drain and cool slightly. Halve each onion lengthways. Melt 1 tablespoon soy spread in a small frying pan. Add the onions, cut-side-down and cook over medium heat for 3–4 minutes, or until well browned. Boil 400 g frozen soy beans for 3 minutes, or until tender, adding 100 g snow peas in the last minute. Drain. Toss together with the onions, 1 tablespoon soy spread and 1 teaspoon soy sauce.

CAULIFLOWER CHEESE

Boil 500 g cauliflower florets for 6 minutes, or until just tender. Drain. Preheat the oven to moderately hot 200°C (400°F/Gas 6). Melt 2 tablespoons soy spread in a saucepan, stir in 4 tablespoons soy flour and cook over medium heat for 1 minute. Take off the heat and whisk in 1 1/2 cups (375 ml) soy milk. Return to the heat and simmer, stirring, for 5 minutes, or until slightly thickened. Stir in 200 g grated soy cheese and 1/2 cup (50 g) grated fresh Parmesan until melted, then add 2 teaspoons Dijon mustard, 2 finely chopped spring onions and a pinch of cayenne pepper. Season. Place the cauliflower in a greased 1.5 litre rectangular ovenproof dish. Pour on the cheese sauce and sprinkle with combined 1/3 cup (40 g) grated soy cheese and 1/4 cup (25 g) grated fresh Parmesan. Bake for 25 minutes, or until golden.

SOY FOR VEGETARIANS

Fresh or dried soy beans and soy-based products such as tofu and tempeh are a great source of protein for vegetarians. Tofu is popularly used in stir-fries or grilled on skewers with vegetables. For something a little more creative, why not try our Individual Tempeh Lasagne, Tofu Fajitas or Tempeh and Mushroom Loaf with Garlic Mash.

TOFU WITH ASIAN GREENS AND SHIITAKE MUSHROOMS

SERVES 4

Kelp and dried bonito flakes are combined to make the all-purpose Japanese sea stock 'dashi'. The kelp acts as a flavour enhancer and was, in fact, what the Japanese first extracted MSG from.

Preparation time: 15 minutes
Total cooking time: 20 minutes

1/3 cup (80 ml) vegetable oil
1 clove garlic, chopped
1 teaspoon grated fresh ginger
60 g shiitake mushrooms, sliced
2 teaspoons dashi powder
3 tablespoons mushroom soy sauce
3 tablespoons mirin
1 teaspoon sugar
2 tablespoons cornflour
2 x 300 g silken firm tofu, each block
    cut into 4 slices
250 g bok choy, chopped
150 g choy sum, chopped
2 spring onions, cut on the diagonal
wasabi, to serve

1 Heat 1 tablespoon of the oil in a saucepan. Add the garlic, ginger and mushrooms and cook for 1–2 minutes, or until softened. Add the dashi powder and 2 cups (500 ml) water. Bring to the boil, reduce the heat and simmer for 5 minutes.

2 Add the soy sauce, mirin and sugar and stir until the sugar has dissolved. Combine the cornflour with a little water to make a smooth paste. Add to the liquid and stir until thickened.

3 Heat 2 tablespoons of the oil in a frying pan. Add the tofu and cook in batches for 2–3 minutes, or until just cooked. Remove from the pan and keep warm. Heat the remaining oil, add the bok choy, choy sum and spring onions and cook for 2 minutes, or until the greens are wilted.

4 Place the greens in a bowl, top with the tofu and pour on the dashi sauce. Serve with rice and a little wasabi on the side.

TOFU FAJITAS

SERVES 4

This dish demonstrates that tofu isn't just for stir-fries and other Asian dishes—it can easily be adapted to fit into other cuisines such as Mexican and Italian.

Preparation time: 25 minutes
Total cooking time: 20 minutes

4 tablespoons light soy sauce
2 cloves garlic, crushed
400 g smoked tofu, cut into
   5 cm strips
200 g canned tomatoes
1 small onion, roughly chopped
1 small fresh red chilli, seeded and
   finely chopped
3 tablespoons chopped fresh
   coriander leaves

1 large ripe avocado
2 teaspoons lemon juice
1 cup (250 g) sour cream
2 tablespoons soy bean oil
1 red capsicum, seeded and sliced
1 yellow capsicum, seeded and
   sliced
8 spring onions, cut into
   5 cm lengths
8 large (15 cm) flour tortillas

1 Place the soy sauce, garlic and 1 teaspoon freshly ground black pepper in a shallow ceramic dish. Add the tofu and toss together well. Cover and leave to marinate.

2 Combine the tomatoes, onion, chilli and coriander in a food processor until smooth. Season with salt and freshly ground black pepper. Transfer to a small saucepan, bring to the boil, then reduce the heat and simmer for 10 minutes. Allow to cool.

3 To make the guacamole, halve the avocado and remove the stone. Scoop the flesh into a bowl and add the lemon juice and 2 tablespoons of the sour cream. Season to taste, then mash well with a fork.

4 Heat 1 tablespoon oil in a frying pan. Add the tofu and any remaining marinade and cook over high heat for 4–5 minutes. Remove from the pan. Heat another 1 tablespoon oil in the pan, add the red and yellow capsicum and spring onion, season and cook for 3–4 minutes.

5 Cook the tortillas quickly in a dry clean frying pan over high heat for 5 seconds on each side.

6 To serve, spread a tortilla with a little guacamole, salsa and sour cream. Top with some tofu and vegetables, fold in one end and roll. Repeat with the remaining tortillas and fillings.

SWEET AND SOUR TOFU

SERVES 4

Most people associate this classic dish with pork, but why not try it with tofu? The subtle flavours of tofu mean this popular sauce is not overpowered.

Preparation time: 15 minutes
Total cooking time: 20 minutes

600 g firm tofu
3–4 tablespoons soy bean oil
100 g snow peas
1 large carrot, julienned
2 cups (150 g) trimmed bean sprouts
   or soy bean sprouts
1 cup (95 g) sliced button mushrooms
6–8 spring onions, cut diagonally
1/3 cup (80 ml) rice vinegar
2 tablespoons light soy sauce
1 1/2 tablespoons caster sugar
2 tablespoons tomato sauce
1 1/2 cups (375 ml) chicken stock
1 tablespoon cornflour

1 Cut the tofu in half horizontally, then cut into triangles—16 in total. Heat 2 tablespoons of the oil in a frying pan. Add the tofu and cook for 2 minutes on each side, or until crisp and golden. Drain on paper towels and keep warm. Wipe the pan clean.

2 Heat the remaining oil. Cut the snow peas in half on the diagonal. Add to the pan with the carrot, bean sprouts, mushrooms and spring onion and stir-fry for 1 minute. Add the rice vinegar, soy sauce, caster sugar, tomato sauce and chicken stock and cook for a further 1 minute.

3 Combine the cornflour with 2 tablespoons water. Add to the vegetables and cook until the sauce thickens. Divide the tofu among the serving bowls and spoon some sauce over the top. Serve with steamed rice on the side.

HONEYED TOFU

SERVES 4

This dish is delicious served with steamed rice or as part of an Asian banquet.

Preparation time: 10 minutes +
   20 minutes standing
Total cooking time: 10 minutes

500 g firm tofu, cut into 1.5 cm cubes
1 teaspoon ground Sichuan pepper
3/4 cup (90 g) plain flour
1/4 cup (20 g) soy flour
1 teaspoon baking powder
1 egg
1 1/4 cups (310 ml) soda water
oil, for deep frying
3 tablespoons honey
2 teaspoons sesame seeds

1 Drain the tofu on paper towels, then season with the Sichuan pepper and some salt. Sift the flours and baking powder together into a bowl, then add a pinch salt. Gradually whisk in the combined egg and soda water, until smooth. Allow to stand for 20 minutes.

2 Fill a heavy-based saucepan or wok one third full of oil and heat to 180°C (350°F), or until a cube of bread browns in 15 seconds. Dip the cubes of tofu in the batter, then cook in the hot oil in batches for 3 minutes, or until lightly golden. Wipe the pan clean.

3 Heat the honey until warmed and liquid. Return the tofu to the pan and toss to coat. Place in a serving dish and sprinkle with the sesame seeds.

SWEET AND SOUR TOFU

SHIITAKE MUSHROOM AND FRESH
SOY BEAN RISOTTO

SERVES 4

Arborio rice is the special rice used for risottos and has a soft texture and chalky centre. During cooking some of the starch from the rice is released, creating the dish's desired creaminess.

Preparation time: 15 minutes +
    20 minutes soaking
Total cooking time: 40 minutes

10 g sliced dried shiitake
    mushrooms
1 cup (160 g) frozen soy beans
3 cups (750 ml) vegetable stock
3 tablespoons soy spread or
    margarine
1 onion, finely diced
1 cup (220 g) arborio rice
1/2 cup (125 ml) white wine
1/2 teaspoon ground white pepper
1/2 cup (50 g) grated fresh
    Parmesan
1 tablespoon chopped fresh parsley

1 Soak the shiitake mushrooms in 1 cup (250 ml) water for 20 minutes. Drain and reserve the liquid. Cook the soy beans in a saucepan of boiling water for 2 minutes. Drain. Place the stock and reserved mushroom liquid in a saucepan and keep at a simmer over low heat.

2 Melt the soy spread in a saucepan. Add the onion and cook over low heat for 5 minutes, or until soft. Increase the heat to medium, add the rice and stir to coat. Pour in the wine and season with salt and white pepper. Cook for a further 2 minutes, or until the wine has been absorbed.

3 Add 1/4 cup (60 ml) of the liquid and stir constantly. Continue adding the liquid, 1/4 cup (60 ml) at a time, stirring constantly, until the liquid has been absorbed after each addition. With the last 1/4 cup (60 ml) liquid, add the soy beans and mushrooms, and cook for a further 2 minutes. Stir in the Parmesan and serve garnished with the parsley.

SOY PASTA WITH MEDITERRANEAN VEGETABLES AND TOFU

SERVES 4–6

Extra virgin olive oil is the highest quality oil, made from the first pressing of olives. It has an intense, fruity flavour and is light and yellowish in colour.

Preparation time: 25 minutes
Total cooking time: 15 minutes

300 g firm tofu, cut into 1 cm cubes
100 ml extra virgin olive oil
1 tablespoon finely chopped fresh
    basil
1 tablespoon finely chopped fresh
    oregano
2 large cloves garlic, finely chopped
1 red onion, thinly sliced
250 g soy pasta
2 tablespoons olive oil
1 eggplant, cut into 2 cm cubes
1 zucchini, cut into 1 cm slices
6 tomatoes, seeded and diced
70 g whole pitted Kalamata olives
fresh basil, to serve

1 Place the tofu in a large bowl. Add the extra virgin olive oil, basil, oregano, garlic, onion, 2 teaspoons salt and 1 teaspoon freshly ground black pepper and stir to coat.

2 Cook the pasta in a large saucepan of boiling water for 10 minutes, or until *al dente*. Keep warm.

3 Meanwhile, heat the olive oil in a large frying pan. Add the eggplant and cook over medium heat for 4 minutes. Season with salt and freshly ground black pepper. Add the zucchini and cook for 6 minutes. Add the tomato and cook for a further 1 minute.

4 Add the tofu mixture to the pan and stir until heated through. Combine with the olives and pasta and serve, garnished with basil.

BEER-BATTERED TEMPEH WITH WEDGES AND AVOCADO AIOLI

SERVES 4

Avocado aïoli is a variation on the traditional garlicky mayonnaise savoured in France, which is often served cold with vegetables, poached chicken or fish.

Preparation time: 20 minutes
Total cooking time: 40 minutes

4 potatoes (600 g), each cut into
    8 wedges
2 tablespoons soy bean oil
1/2 cup (65 g) besan (chickpea
    flour)
2 tablespoons soy flour
2 tablespoons cumin seeds,
    toasted and ground
2 tablespoons coriander seeds,
    toasted and ground
1 tablespoon sweet paprika
    powder
2/3 cup (170 ml) beer
vegetable oil, for deep-frying
600 g tempeh, cut into 12 fingers
    (10 x 2 cm)

fresh coriander leaves, to garnish,
    optional
spring onions, sliced, to garnish,
    optional

AVOCADO AIOLI
1/2 cup (15 g) fresh coriander
    leaves
1 clove garlic, crushed
1/4 cup (60 ml) extra virgin olive oil
1/2 teaspoon chilli flakes
1/2 tablespoon lemon juice
1 fresh jalapeño chilli, finely
    chopped
1 medium or 1/2 large avocado,
    chopped

1 Preheat the oven to moderate 180°C (350°F/Gas 4). Place the potato wedges on a baking tray, drizzle with the soy bean oil and season with salt and pepper. Toss to coat well. Bake for 40 minutes, or until golden brown.

2 Meanwhile, to make the avocado aïoli, combine the coriander leaves, garlic, oil, chilli flakes, lemon juice, chilli, avocado and 1 teaspoon salt in a food processor until smooth.

3 Place the chickpea and soy flours, cumin, coriander, paprika, beer and 1 teaspoon salt in a bowl and mix to a medium thick batter.

4 Fill a deep heavy-based saucepan one third full with oil and heat to warm 170°C (325°F), or until a cube of bread browns in 20 seconds.

5 Dip the slices of tempeh in the batter, then deep-fry for 1 minute, or until golden. Drain on crumpled paper towels. Serve with the wedges and aïoli on the side. Garnish with the coriander leaves and spring onion, if desired.

TOFU AND SPINACH CANNELLONI
WITH FRESH TOMATO SAUCE

SERVES 6-8

Cannelloni can be enjoyed on its own as an entrée or with a fresh green salad as a main course. Tofu replaces the traditional ricotta in the filling without the loss of protein or calcium.

Preparation time: 50 minutes
Total cooking time: 1 hour 15 minutes

2 tablespoons soy bean oil
1 onion, chopped
2 cloves garlic, crushed
1/4 cup (60 g) tomato paste
950 g tomatoes, seeded and diced
1 teaspoon sugar
1 1/2 cup (375 ml) vegetable stock
1 tablespoon finely chopped fresh
  basil
1 tablespoon finely chopped fresh
  oregano
270 g cannelloni tubes
grated Parmesan, to garnish

FILLING
300 g chopped fresh English
  spinach
500 g firm tofu, mashed
3/4 cup (75 g) grated Parmesan
1/2 cup (80 g) pine nuts, toasted

BECHAMEL
3 tablespoons soy spread or
  margarine
5 tablespoons plain flour
1 litre malt-free soy milk
1/2 teaspoon ground nutmeg

1 Preheat the oven to moderately hot 200°C (400°F/Gas 6). Heat the oil in a saucepan over medium heat. Add the onion and garlic, cook for 3 minutes, then stir in the tomato paste. Cook for 2 minutes. Add the tomato and sugar and cook, stirring frequently, for 4 minutes. Gradually add the stock and bring to the boil, then simmer for 25 minutes, or until thickened. Remove from the heat and stir in the basil and oregano.

2 To make the filling, steam the spinach for 3 minutes, or until wilted. Allow to cool, then squeeze out any excess water. Combine the spinach, tofu, Parmesan and 1/4 cup (40 g) of the pine nuts in a bowl. Season with salt and freshly ground black pepper.

3 To make the béchamel, melt the soy spread in a saucepan. Add the flour and cook, stirring constantly, over medium heat for 2 minutes. Reduce the heat and gradually whisk in the milk. Add the nutmeg and season. Simmer, stirring constantly, for 5 minutes, or until the sauce thickens.

4 Pour half the tomato sauce and half the béchamel over the base of a large rectangular 30 x 21 x 5 cm ovenproof dish. Spoon the tofu filling into the cannelloni tubes and arrange in the dish. Pour the remaining tomato sauce over the cannelloni, followed by the béchamel, then sprinkle the remaining pine nuts on top. Bake for 30 minutes, or until bubbling and lightly golden. Garnish with the grated Parmesan.

TOFU IN BLACK BEAN SAUCE

SERVES 4

Fermented black beans have a strong flavour, but the black bean sauce itself prepared from this variety of soy beans is quite delicate in comparison.

Preparation time: 20 minutes
Total cooking time: 15 minutes

1/3 cup (80 ml) vegetable stock
2 teaspoons cornflour
2 teaspoons Chinese rice wine
1 teaspoon sesame oil
1 tablespoon soy sauce
2 tablespoons peanut oil
450 g firm tofu, cut into 2 cm cubes
2 cloves garlic, very finely chopped
2 teaspoons finely chopped fresh
   ginger
3 tablespoons fermented black beans,
   rinsed and very finely chopped
4 spring onions, cut on the diagonal
   (white and green parts)
1 red capsicum, cut into
   2 cm chunks
300 g baby bok choy, chopped
   crossways into 2 cm pieces

1 Combine the vegetable stock, cornflour, Chinese rice wine, sesame oil, soy sauce, 1/2 teaspoon salt and freshly ground black pepper in a small bowl.

2 Heat a wok over medium heat, add the peanut oil and swirl to coat. Add the tofu and stir-fry in two batches for 3 minutes each batch, or until lightly browned. Remove with a slotted spoon and drain on paper towels. Remove any bits of tofu stuck to the wok or floating in the oil.

3 Add the garlic and ginger, and stir-fry for 30 seconds. Add the black beans and spring onion, and cook for 30 seconds, then stir in capsicum for 1 minute. Add the bok choy and stir-fry for a further 2 minutes. Return the tofu to the wok and stir gently. Pour in the sauce and stir for 2–3 minutes, or until the sauce has thickened slightly. Serve immediately with steamed rice.

TEMPEH AND MUSHROOM LOAF WITH GARLIC MASH

SERVES 4

Filled with tempeh, mushrooms and nuts, this dish is not only similar to 'meatloaf' in shape, it contains the meat-like proteins for vegetarians.

Preparation time: 40 minutes
Total cooking time: 50 minutes

1 tablespoon soy bean oil
1 onion, finely chopped
250 g field mushrooms, finely
    chopped
1 cup (155 g) brazil nuts, roasted
1 cup (155 g) unsalted roasted
    cashews
300 g seasoned tempeh, roughly
    chopped
1½ cups (120 g) fresh breadcrumbs
100 g onion and garlic flavoured
    soy cheese, grated
¼ teaspoon dried mixed herbs
1 egg, lightly beaten

GARLIC MASH
1 kg potatoes, chopped
2 cups (500 ml) vegetable stock
1 clove garlic, crushed
1 teaspoon butter
2 tablespoons cream
white pepper, to season

TOMATO SAUCE
1 tablespoon soy bean oil
1 small onion, finely chopped
1 clove garlic
400 g can chopped tomatoes
1–2 teaspoons sugar
2 teaspoons balsamic vinegar
1 teaspoon chopped fresh oregano

1 Preheat the oven to moderate 180°C (350°F/Gas 4). Grease a 10 x 22 cm loaf tin and line the base with baking paper. Heat the oil in a large frying pan. Add the onion and mushrooms and cook for 5 minutes, or until soft and the liquid has evaporated. Allow to cool.

2 Grind the brazil nuts and cashews in a food processor for 10–15 seconds—ensure they are not too finely ground. Transfer to a large bowl. Process the tempeh for 15 seconds, or until coarsely ground. Add to the nuts, along with the mushroom mixture, breadcrumbs, soy cheese, mixed herbs and egg. Season with salt and freshly ground black pepper. Mix together with your hands until well combined. Spoon into the prepared tin and press down the surface. Bake for 45 minutes, or until firm.

3 To make the garlic mash, place the potato in a large saucepan. Add the stock and enough water to cover—about 1 cup (250 ml). Bring to the boil, then reduce the heat and simmer for 15–20 minutes, or until soft. Drain, reserving ⅓ cup (80 ml) of the cooking liquid. Mash the potato, then mix in the garlic, butter, cream and reserved cooking liquid. Season with salt and white pepper.

4 To make the sauce, heat the oil in a saucepan. Add the onion and cook for 2 minutes, or until soft, taking care not to brown. Add the garlic and cook a further 1 minute. Add the tomatoes with any liquid and bring to the boil. Reduce the heat, add the sugar and vinegar and simmer for 8–10 minutes, or until reduced and thickened. Add the chopped oregano and simmer for another 2 minutes.

5 To serve, slice the tempeh loaf, top with the sauce and dollop some mash on the side.

PEANUT AND LIME-CRUSTED TOFU WITH CHILLI JAM

SERVES 4

The kaffir lime (or makrut lime) is a knobbly, dark-skinned fruit with a strong lime fragrance and flavour. Commonly used in soups and curries, here it is incorporated into a batter and deep-fried.

Preparation time: 15 minutes
Total cooking time: 15 minutes

¼ cup (30 g) besan (chickpea flour)
2 tablespoons soy flour
2 tablespoons soy sauce
2 tablespoons peanut butter
1 fresh kaffir lime leaf, finely
   shredded
500 g firm tofu, cut into 2 cm
   slices
peanut oil, for deep-frying
600 g bok choy, quartered
   lengthways
1 tablespoon purchased chilli jam
fresh kaffir lime leaf, shredded,
   extra, to garnish

1 Combine the besan and soy flours, soy sauce, peanut butter, shredded lime leaf and 2 teaspoons salt in a bowl. Slowly add 100 ml water, stirring constantly, until the batter reaches a medium thick consistency.

2 Fill a saucepan one third full of oil and heat to 190°C (375°F), or until a cube of bread browns in 10 seconds. Quickly dip 2–3 slices of the tofu in the batter and deep-fry for 2 minutes, or until golden brown. Drain on paper towels. Repeat with the remaining tofu slices and batter.

3 Steam the bok choy in a saucepan for 2–3 minutes, or until tender but still bright green. Divide the greens among the serving plates, arrange three pieces of tofu on top, dollop with a teaspoon of chilli jam and garnish with the extra shredded kaffir lime leaf.

TOFU STROGANOFF

SERVES 4

This dish can easily be adapted to the traditional beef stroganoff—simply shallow-fry strips of fillet steak instead of the tofu.

Preparation time: 20 minutes
Total cooking time: 30 minutes

2 tablespoons plain flour
1 tablespoon paprika
500 g firm tofu, cut into
    1.5 cm cubes
1 tablespoon soy bean oil
2 teaspoons tomato paste
¼ cup (60 ml) dry sherry
2 cups (500 ml) vegetable stock
12 pickling onions, halved
1 clove garlic, crushed
225 g field mushrooms, cut into
    1 cm slices
3 tablespoons sour cream
sour cream, extra, to garnish
2 tablespoons chopped fresh chives

1 Place the flour and paprika in a plastic bag and season well with salt and freshly ground black pepper. Add the tofu and shake well to coat.

2 Heat the soy bean oil in a frying pan. Add the tofu and cook until golden all over. Add the tomato paste and cook for a further 1 minute. Add 2 tablespoons of the sherry, cook for 30 seconds then transfer to a bowl. Keep any remaining flour in the pan—do not wipe clean.

3 Pour 1 cup (250 ml) of the stock into the pan and bring to the boil. Add the onion, garlic and mushrooms, reduce the heat to medium and simmer, covered, for 10 minutes.

4 Return the tofu to the pan with the remaining sherry and remaining stock. Season to taste with salt and freshly ground black pepper. Return to the boil, reduce the heat to medium, then simmer for 5 minutes, or until heated through and the sauce has thickened.

5 Remove the pan from the heat and stir in a little of the sauce into the sour cream until smooth and of pouring consistency. Pour the sour cream mixture back into the pan—this technique prevents the sour cream from separating and will give the sauce a smoother consistency.

6 Garnish with a dollop of the extra sour cream and sprinkle with the chopped chives. Serve with noodles or steamed rice.

MEDITERRANEAN PIZZA

SERVES 4

Yeast is sensitive to drafts, so ensure you leave the yeast to rise in a warm, draft-free place when foaming and allowing the dough to rise.

Preparation time: 30 minutes +
   35 minutes rising
Total cooking time: 25 minutes

7 g sachet dried yeast
1 teaspoon sugar
2¼ cups (280 g) plain flour
½ cup (40 g) soy flour
soy oil, for greasing
1½ tablespoons purchased
   sun-dried tomato pesto
100 g soy cheese, grated
⅓ cup (35 g) grated tasty cheese
1 small red capsicum, thinly sliced
½ red onion, thinly sliced
2 tablespoons pine nuts
10 pitted black olives
fresh basil leaves, to garnish

1 To make the pizza base, place the yeast, sugar, ½ teaspoon salt and 1 cup (250 ml) warm water in a bowl and stir until dissolved. Cover with plastic wrap and leave in a warm place for 10 minutes, or until bubbles appear on the surface. The mixture should be frothy and slightly increased in volume. If your yeast doesn't foam it is dead, so you will have to discard it and start again.

2 Sift the plain and soy flours into a large bowl. Make a well in the centre and add the yeast mixture. Mix to form a dough. Knead the dough on a lightly floured surface for 10 minutes, or until smooth and elastic. Cover and set aside in a warm place for 25 minutes, or until doubled in size.

3 Preheat the oven to moderately hot 200°C (400°F/Gas 6). Grease a 30 cm pizza tray. Roll out the dough on a lightly floured surface to a 34 cm circle, transfer to the prepared pizza tray and fold over the edge and press down.

4 Spread the base with the sun-dried tomato pesto and sprinkle with the combined soy and tasty cheeses. Top with the capsicum, onion, pine nuts and olives. Season with black pepper. Bake for 20–25 minutes, or until golden brown. Garnish with the basil leaves and cut into wedges to serve.

EGGPLANT STUFFED WITH SOY BEANS AND VEGETABLES

SERVES 4

Enjoyed now around the world, the eggplant (or aubergine) originated in India. It is common in the Middle East to serve eggplants filled with vegetables, such as this.

Preparation time: 30 minutes
Total cooking time: 1 hour 35 minutes

2 x 350 g eggplants
2 tablespoons soy bean oil
1 onion, chopped
2 cloves garlic, crushed
1 celery stick, finely chopped
415 g can diced tomatoes
1 1/2 tablespoons tomato paste
1/2 cup (125 ml) white wine
3/4 cup (185 ml) vegetable stock or
    water
300 g can soy beans, rinsed and
    drained
1/2 teaspoon sugar
3/4 cup (45 g) chopped fresh parsley
100 g soy cheese, grated
3/4 cup (75 g) coarsely grated
    Parmesan

1 Preheat the oven to moderate 180°C (350°F/Gas 4). Pour 1/2 cup (125 ml) water into an ovenproof ceramic dish and set aside. Halve the eggplants lengthways and scoop out the flesh with a spoon, leaving a 1 cm border. Dice the flesh. Arrange the shells in the prepared dish.

2 Heat the oil in a large frying pan. Add the onion, garlic and celery and cook over medium heat for 5 minutes, or until softened. Add the diced eggplant flesh and cook, stirring frequently, for a further 10 minutes, or until the eggplant is tender. Add the tomato, tomato paste, wine and stock and cook, stirring, for 8 minutes, or until reduced slightly. Season with salt and pepper. Add the soy beans, sugar and 1/2 cup (30 g) of the parsley and cook for a further 5 minutes. Stir in the soy cheese and 1/2 cup (50 g) of the Parmesan.

3 Spoon the filling firmly into the eggplant shells. Use pieces of foil to prop up the outer walls if necessary. Cover loosely with foil, and bake for 1 hour, or until the flesh of the eggplant shell is cooked.

4 Remove the foil and sprinkle with the remaining Parmesan. Cook under a hot grill for 2–3 minutes, or until golden. Sprinkle with the remaining parsley and serve hot.

SOY BEAN ENCHILADAS

Enchiladas are a popular Mexican dish—tortillas are dipped in a tomato sauce, fried then filled, rolled up and then baked. This recipe uses soy beans instead of the traditional kidney beans.

Preparation time: 35 minutes
Total cooking time: 1 hour

SAUCE
2 teaspoons soy bean oil
1 onion, finely chopped
2 cloves garlic, crushed
1 teaspoon ground cumin
1 teaspoon ground coriander
1/2 teaspoon chilli powder
400 g can puréed tomato
1/2 cup (125 ml) vegetable stock
1 teaspoon sugar

550 g butternut pumpkin, peeled
    and seeded
2 teaspoons soy bean oil
1 onion, finely chopped
1 teaspoon chilli powder
425 g can diced tomato
300 g can soy beans, rinsed and
    drained
200 g can corn kernels, drained
8 large corn tortillas
100 g soy cheese, grated
chopped fresh parsley, to garnish

1 Preheat the oven to moderate 180°C (350°F/Gas 4). Grease a 22 x 32 x 6 cm ovenproof ceramic dish.

2 To make the sauce, heat the oil in a saucepan. Add the onion and cook over medium heat for 3 minutes, or until soft. Add the garlic, ground cumin, ground coriander and chilli powder. Cook, stirring, for 1 minute. Add the puréed tomato and stock and bring to the boil. Reduce the heat and simmer for 5 minutes. Add the sugar and season to taste with salt and freshly ground black pepper.

3 To make the filling, cut the pumpkin into 1.5 cm cubes. Steam for 12 minutes, or until just tender. Heat the oil in a saucepan, add the onion and cook over medium heat for 3 minutes, or until soft. Add the chilli powder, cook for 30 seconds, then add the tomato and simmer for 15 minutes, or until pulpy. Add the pumpkin, soy beans and corn and stir to combine.

4 Working one at a time, dip a tortilla into the sauce to coat both sides, then put about 1/3 cup of the filling across the centre and roll up to enclose—it is easier if you do this in the prepared dish. Place the enchilada, seam-side-down, at one end of the dish. Repeat with the remaining filling and tortillas, lining them up close together in the dish.

5 Pour the remaining sauce over the enchiladas and sprinkle with the cheese. Bake for 20–25 minutes, or until the cheese has melted. Sprinkle with parsley and serve immediately, with a green salad.

SOY PASTA WITH CREAMY MUSHROOM AND LEEK SAUCE

SERVES 4–6

Leeks are considered 'poor man's asparagus' in France, but there's nothing poor about this deliciously rich sauce. Before cooking with leeks, make sure you wash the dirt out from between the leaves.

Preparation time: 15 minutes
Total cooking time: 25 minutes

2 leeks
1 tablespoon soy spread or margarine
2 tablespoons soy bean oil
250 g button mushrooms
375 g soy pasta
150 g silken tofu, drained
100 ml cream
2 tablespoons grated fresh Parmesan
1 teaspoon fresh thyme, chopped
grated fresh Parmesan, extra,
    to serve
fresh thyme sprigs, to garnish

1 Wash the leeks thoroughly. Cut each in half lengthways and thinly slice. Heat the soy spread and 1 tablespoon of the oil in a large saucepan. Add the leek and gently cook for 10–12 minutes, or until soft—do not brown. Add the remaining oil, then stir in the mushrooms. Cook for 7–10 minutes, or until soft. Remove from the heat and cover to keep warm.

2 Meanwhile, cook the pasta in a large saucepan of boiling water until *al dente*. Drain. Keep warm.

3 Combine the tofu, cream, Parmesan and thyme in a food processor until smooth. Season with salt and freshly ground black pepper.

4 Return the pan to the heat and add the tofu cream mixture. Gently cook for 2–3 minutes, or until warmed through. Serve the pasta topped with the sauce and garnish with the extra Parmesan and thyme sprigs.

SWEET POTATO GNOCCHI WITH ROAST EGGPLANT

SERVES 4

Gnocchi are small Italian dumplings related to pasta. Traditionally, they are made from a mixture of potato flour and wheat flour, or from semolina or polenta.

Preparation time: 45 minutes
Total cooking time: 50 minutes

500 g eggplant, cut into 2 cm cubes
1 tablespoon olive oil
1 large clove garlic, crushed
750 g orange sweet potato, peeled
    and cut into 3 cm chunks
250 g firm tofu
1 cup (125 g) plain flour
1 egg yolk
50 g soy spread
1 tablespoon fresh thyme leaves
2 tablespoons chopped fresh parsley
shaved Parmesan, to garnish
fresh thyme sprigs, to garnish

1 Preheat the oven to hot 200°C (400°F/Gas 6). Place the eggplant, oil and garlic in a bowl and toss together until well coated. Transfer to a baking tray. Bake for 20 minutes, or until browned and cooked through.

2 Meanwhile, steam the orange sweet potato for 10 minutes, or until tender. Drain and pat dry. Transfer to a bowl and mash with a potato masher. Drain the tofu well and gently pat dry with a clean cloth. Add to the orange sweet potato and mash together well. Add the flour and egg yolk and stir through. Season with salt and freshly ground black pepper.

3 Turn the dough out onto a lightly floured surface, adding more flour if the mixture is too sticky—do not overwork or it will become gluey. Bring the dough together into a ball with your hands.

4 Divide the dough into four portions and roll each portion on a lightly floured surface, to form a sausage shape about 2 cm in diameter. Cut into 2.5 cm pieces and shape each piece into an oval. Press each oval against a floured fork. As you make the gnocchi place them in a single layer on a baking tray, and cover until ready to cook.

5 Melt the soy spread in a small saucepan over medium heat. Add the thyme and cook, stirring, over low heat for 2 minutes.

6 Bring a large saucepan of salted water to the boil and cook the gnocchi in batches, for 3–4 minutes, or until the gnocchi rise to the surface. Remove with a slotted spoon and keep warm.

7 Add the eggplant and the parsley to the thyme mixture return, the pan to the heat and warm through for 2–3 minutes over medium heat. Season. Divide the gnocchi among serving bowls, top with the eggplant mixture and garnish with Parmesan shavings and thyme sprigs.

MACARONI CHEESE

SERVES 4

Macaroni is the Anglicised version of the Italian maccheroni, *a tubular form of pasta. But, in both Italian and English it is also used as a generic term for pasta (excluding sheet and filled pasta).*

Preparation time: 10 minutes
Total cooking time: 30 minutes

500 g soy pasta twists
50 g soy spread
6 spring onions, finely sliced
1 tablespoon soy flour
1 litre soy milk
2 tablespoons cornflour dissolved
    in 2–3 tablespoons water
1 bay leaf
2 1/2 cups (310 g) grated vintage
    Cheddar
1 teaspoon paprika
1 tablespoon finely chopped fresh
    parsley

1　Preheat the oven to moderately hot 200°C (400°F/Gas 6). Cook the soy pasta in a large saucepan of boiling water until *al dente*. Drain and transfer to a large bowl.

2　Meanwhile, melt the soy spread in a saucepan over medium heat. Add the spring onion and cook for 1–2 minutes, or until soft. Add the soy flour and cook, stirring, for 2 minutes. Remove the pan from the heat and whisk in the soy milk and cornflour mixture until the sauce is smooth.

3　Return to the heat, add the bay leaf and bring to the boil, stirring constantly. Reduce the heat and simmer, stirring for 3 minutes. Remove the bay leaf and stir in 2 cups (250 g) of the cheese. Season well with salt and freshly ground black pepper. Pour the sauce over the pasta and mix together until well coated.

4　Spoon into a 3 litre ovenproof baking dish and sprinkle with the remaining cheese. Bake for 15 minutes, or until golden brown. Sprinkle with the paprika and parsley and serve immediately.

BLACK BEAN PANCAKES WITH BOK CHOY

SERVES 4

When buying the ingredients for these pancakes, make sure you buy the black soy beans which are fermented and salted, not the Mexican black beans which are quite different.

Preparation time: 30 minutes +
    10 minutes soaking
Total cooking time: 20 minutes

250 g baby bok choy, cut into
    quarters
1/2 cup (60 g) fermented black
    beans
3/4 cup (90 g) plain flour
3/4 cup (60 g) soy flour
1 teaspoon baking powder
4 eggs, lightly beaten
3/4 cup (185 ml) soy milk
1 cup (90 g) bean sprouts or soy
    bean sprouts
4 spring onions, thinly sliced
1/2 cup (25 g) fresh coriander leaves,
    finely chopped
1 tablespoon finely chopped fresh
    ginger
3 cloves garlic, finely chopped
2 small fresh red chillies, finely
    chopped
1 tablespoon sherry
3 tablespoons soy bean oil
1 clove garlic, crushed
sweet chilli sauce, to serve

1 Bring a large saucepan of salted water to the boil. Add the bok choy and cook for 2 minutes. Drain and plunge into ice-cold water. Soak the black beans in water for 10 minutes. Drain.

2 Sift the flours and baking powder into a bowl and make a well in the centre. Combine the egg and milk, then whisk into the flour mixture until it forms a smooth paste. Add the black beans, sprouts, spring onion, coriander, ginger, garlic, chilli and sherry and mix well.

3 Heat 1/2 tablespoon soy bean oil in a large frying pan, wiping the surface lightly with paper towels to remove any excess oil. When hot, add 1/3 cup (80 ml) of the batter, spreading out to form a 10 cm wide pancake (depending on the size of your pan, you should be able to cook two or three at a time). Cook over medium heat for 1–2 minutes, or until small bubbles appear on the surface and the underneath is golden brown. Turn and cook for a further minute. Remove and keep warm. Repeat with the remaining batter to make 8 pancakes—add an extra 1/2 tablespoon oil, if necessary.

4 Heat the remaining soy bean oil in a frying pan or wok. Add the bok choy and stir-fry over medium heat for 2 minutes. Add the crushed garlic and cook for a further minute. Season well with salt and freshly ground black pepper. Arrange two pancakes on a serving plate, top with the bok choy and dollop with sweet chilli sauce on the side.

TOFU KEBABS WITH ASIAN MISO PESTO

SERVES 4

For these kebabs, influences are borrowed from a number of popular cuisines (Chinese, Japanese, Italian) to produce an amazing taste sensation.

Preparation time: 30 minutes +
   1 hour marinating
Total cooking time: 10 minutes

1 large red capsicum, cut into
   squares
12 button mushrooms, halved
6 pickling onions, quartered
3 zucchini, cut into 3 cm chunks
450 g firm tofu, cut into
   2 cm cubes
1/2 cup (125 ml) light olive oil
1/4 cup (60 ml) light soy sauce
2 cloves garlic, crushed
2 teaspoons grated fresh ginger

MISO PESTO
1/2 cup (80 g) unsalted roasted
   peanuts
2 cups (60 g) firmly packed fresh
   coriander leaves
2 tablespoons white miso paste
2 cloves garlic
5 tablespoons olive oil

1 Soak 12 wooden skewers in cold water for 10 minutes. Thread the vegetable pieces and tofu alternately onto the skewers, then place in a large rectangular ceramic dish. Combine the olive oil, soy sauce, garlic and ginger in a small bowl, then pour half the mixture over the kebabs. Cover with plastic wrap and refrigerate for 1 hour.

2 To make the miso pesto, place the peanuts, coriander leaves, miso paste and garlic in a food processor and mix until finely chopped. Slowly add the olive oil while the machine is still running and blend until you have a smooth paste.

3 Heat a grill plate and cook the kebabs, turning and brushing frequently with the remaining marinade, for 4–6 minutes, or until the edges are slightly brown. Serve with steamed rice and a little of the miso pesto.

INDIVIDUAL TEMPEH LASAGNE

SERVES 6

Thin slices of tempeh replace pasta sheets to produce an impressive dinner party dish. If you don't have individual gratin dishes, build each lasagne free-form on a baking tray, then transfer to a serving plate.

Preparation time: 25 minutes
Total cooking time: 40 minutes

4 tablespoons olive oil
1 onion, chopped
3 cloves garlic, chopped
600 g bottled tomato pasta sauce
1/2 cup (80 g) sun-dried tomatoes, drained and finely sliced
1/4 cup (60 ml) dry white wine
1 tablespoon shredded fresh basil
2 x 300 g blocks tempeh, cut lengthways into 3 thin slices, then halved
120 g baby spinach leaves
1 teaspoon chopped garlic, extra
3 cups (450 g) grated mozzarella
fresh basil leaves, to garnish

1 Preheat the oven to moderate 180°C (350°F/Gas 4).

2 Heat 1 tablespoon of the oil in a saucepan. Add the onion and garlic and gently cook for 2 minutes, or until the onion is lightly golden. Add the bottled pasta sauce, sun-dried tomato and white wine. Season to taste with salt and freshly ground black pepper. Cook for 20 minutes, or until thick and pulpy. Cool slightly, then stir in the basil.

3 Heat the remaining oil in a frying pan. Add the tempeh slices and cook for 5–8 minutes, or until crisp and golden. Drain on paper towels. Add the baby spinach to the same frying pan. Add the extra garlic and 1 tablespoon water and cook until the spinach has wilted.

4 Place a slice of tempeh on the bottom of 6 individual gratin dishes. Cover with a little tomato sauce, some spinach and half of the mozzarella. Repeat with another layer of tempeh, sauce, spinach and the remaining mozzarella. Bake for 10–15 minutes, or until golden brown. Garnish with fresh basil leaves and serve with a fresh green salad, if desired.

SOY FOR DINNER

When you think of dinner, do you think of meat and vegetables? If so, does 'Soy for dinner' mean a roast made from tofu? Not at all. We simply incorporate soy-based products such as miso paste, tofu, soy sauce and soy beans to beef, chicken, pork and seafood dishes from a variety of popular cuisines. In this chapter you'll find Miso Yakitori Chicken, Chilli con Carne with Soy Beans, and a Soy Bean Moussaka you'll absolutely love.

BOSTON BAKED SOY BEANS

SERVES 4–6

The Puritan families in and around Boston baked their beans with treacle and spices. Here soy beans are treated to this traditional cooking method.

Preparation time: 15 minutes + overnight soaking
Total cooking time: 5 hours 40 minutes

500 g dried soy beans
2 onions, chopped
1 tablespoon treacle
1/4 cup (55 g) demerara sugar
3 teaspoons dried mustard
2 smoked pork hocks
    (about 600 g each)
2 tablespoons tomato sauce

1 Soak the soy beans in water for 8 hours. Drain. Place in a large saucepan and cover with water. Bring to the boil and simmer for 2 hours—top up with water, if necessary. Drain, reserving 2 cups (500 ml) of the liquid.

2 Preheat the oven to warm 160°C (315°F/Gas 2–3). Place the reserved liquid in a 3.5 litre heavy-based casserole dish. Add the onion, treacle, sugar, mustard and some pepper and bring to the boil. Reduce the heat and simmer for 2 minutes. Add the beans and pork. Bake, covered, for 3 hours, stirring occasionally—keep the beans covered with liquid. Stir in the tomato sauce and bake, uncovered, for 30 minutes. Remove the pork and skim any fat off the surface of the beans. Roughly shred the pork and stir into the beans.

LAMB CUTLETS WITH SOY BEAN SKORDALIA

SERVES 4

Skordalia is a classic garlic sauce that has regional variations. This variation is different again, with the use of soy beans as the base of the sauce instead of soaked and squeezed white bread.

Preparation time: 15 minutes +
    2 hours marinating
Total cooking time: 30 minutes

1 1/2 tablespoons honey
3 tablespoons miso paste
1 tablespoon light soy sauce
4 racks French-trimmed lamb
    (3 cutlets each rack)
4 Roma tomatoes, halved
2 x 400 g cans soy beans, drained
1/2 cup (55 g) ground almonds
1/2 cup (50 g) dried breadcrumbs
2 tablespoons lemon juice
3 cloves garlic
3/4 cup (180 ml) extra virgin olive oil
3/4 cup (185 ml) chicken stock
2 tablespoons chopped fresh chives

1 Combine the honey, miso and soy sauce, then spread over the lamb—do not spread on the bones as they will blacken. Cover and chill for 2 hours.

2 Preheat the oven to moderately hot 200°C (400°F/Gas 6). Place the lamb and the tomatoes in a roasting tin and season the tomatoes. Dizzle with 30 ml oil. Roast for 20–25 minutes, or until the lamb is medium rare. Rest for 5 minutes, then carve the racks into cutlets.

3 Meanwhile, place the beans in a food processor with the ground almonds, breadcrumbs, lemon juice and garlic. Slowly add the remaining olive oil and process until smooth and creamy. Transfer the skordalia to a saucepan and stir in the stock until smooth and warmed through. Divide among four plates, place three cutlets on top and tomatoes on the side. Drizzle with pan juices and garnish with the chives.

BOSTON BAKED SOY BEANS

CHINESE-STYLE STEAMED FISH

SERVES 4

Serve this Asian-flavoured fish dish as a complete meal with steamed rice and your favourite combination of stir-fried vegetables.

Preparation time: 15 minutes +
    4 hours marinating
Total cooking time: 25 minutes

3 tablespoons white miso paste
1 tablespoon soy bean oil
2 cloves garlic, crushed
1½ tablespoons grated fresh
    ginger
2 tablespoons light soy sauce
2 tablespoons oyster sauce
1 large whole red snapper, cleaned
    and scaled (about 1.5 kg)
4 spring onions, sliced on the
    diagonal
fresh coriander leaves, to garnish

1 Combine the miso, soy bean oil, garlic, ginger, soy and oyster sauces in a food processor until smooth. Line a large bamboo steamer with baking paper—this makes it easier to remove the fish. If the fish is too big, cut off the head.

2 Make four deep diagonal slashes across both sides of the fish. Spoon half the paste over one side of the fish and rub well into the skin and slashes. Repeat on the other side with the remaining paste. Place on a plate, cover with plastic wrap and refrigerate for 2–4 hours.

3 Place the fish in the steamer, top with the spring onion and steam over a wok of boiling water for 20–25 minutes, or until the fish is cooked.

4 Remove the fish from the steamer, pour any juices collected in the baking paper over the top and garnish with coriander.

MISO YAKITORI CHICKEN

SERVES 4

Sake is often referred to as a rice wine, but technically it is a beer as it is brewed from grain. Usually drunk warm in small porcelain cups, this alcoholic beverage also adds flavour to marinades and sauces.

Preparation time: 30 minutes
Total cooking time: 20 minutes

3 tablespoons yellow or red
   miso paste
2 tablespoons sugar
1/4 cup (60 ml) sake
2 tablespoons mirin
1 kg chicken thighs, boned (skin on),
   cut into 2.5 cm cubes
1 cucumber, seeded and cut into
   2 cm batons
2 spring onions, cut into 2 cm
   pieces

1 Soak 12 long wooden bamboo skewers in cold water for 10 minutes. Cook the miso, sugar, sake and mirin in a small saucepan over medium heat, stirring well, for 2 minutes, or until smooth and the sugar has dissolved.

2 Thread the chicken, cucumber and spring onion alternately onto the skewers—you should have 3 pieces of each per skewer.

3 Cook on a grill plate over high heat, turning occasionally, for 10 minutes, or until the chicken is almost cooked. Brush with the miso sauce and continue cooking, then turn and brush the other side. Repeat once or twice until cooked. Serve immediately with steamed rice and salad.

MISO YAKITORI CHICKEN BALLS

SERVES 4

This dish is a variation to the above kebabs—chicken mince balls are threaded alternately with spring onion pieces and cooked under the grill.

Preparation time: 10 minutes +
   1 hour chilling
Total cooking time: 12 minutes

500 g minced chicken
3 cloves garlic, crushed
1 tablespoon grated fresh ginger
1 egg yolk
1/2 cup (30 g) Japanese
   breadcrumbs (panko)
6 tablespoons miso paste
2 tablespoons sugar
1/4 cup (60 ml) sake
2 tablespoons mirin
10 spring onions, cut into
   2 cm pieces

1 Soak 12 wooden skewers in cold water for at least 10 minutes. Combine the minced chicken, garlic, ginger, egg yolk, breadcrumbs and half the miso paste with your hands. Roll into walnut-sized balls. Chill for 1 hour.

2 Place the sugar, sake, mirin and remaining miso in a small saucepan over medium heat. Cook, stirring well, for 2 minutes, or until the sauce is smooth and the sugar has completely dissolved.

3 Thread the chicken balls and spring onion alternately onto the skewers— you should have 3 balls and 2 pieces of spring onion per skewer. Brush with the miso glaze, coating each one well.

4 Cook under a medium grill, brushing regularly with the glaze and turning occasionally for 10 minutes, or until the chicken is cooked through.

MISO YAKITORI CHICKEN

THAI-STYLE RED CURRY WITH SEAFOOD AND TOFU

SERVES 4

Kaffir limes, lemon grass, galangal, fresh coriander and coconut milk are traditional Thai ingredients. Mixed with seafood and tofu, this dish will be as good as any from a Thai restaurant.

Preparation time: 30 minutes
Total cooking time: 30 minutes

2 tablespoons soy bean oil
500 g firm white fish (ling, perch), cut into 2 cm cubes
250 g raw prawns, peeled and deveined, tails intact
2 x 400 ml cans coconut milk
1 tablespoon Thai red curry paste
4 fresh or 8 dried kaffir lime leaves
2 tablespoons fish sauce
2 tablespoons finely chopped fresh lemon grass (white part only)
2 cloves garlic, crushed

1 tablespoon finely chopped fresh galangal
1 tablespoon shaved palm sugar
300 g silken firm tofu, cut into 1.5 cm cubes
1/2 cup (60 g) bamboo shoots, julienned
1 large fresh red chilli, finely sliced
2 teaspoons lime juice
spring onions, chopped, to garnish
fresh coriander leaves, chopped, to garnish

1 Heat the oil in a large frying pan or wok. Sear the fish and prawns over medium heat for 1 minute on each side. Remove from the pan.

2 Place 1/4 cup (60 ml) coconut milk and the curry paste in the pan and cook over medium heat for 2 minutes, or until fragrant and the oil separates. Add the kaffir lime leaves, fish sauce, lemon grass, garlic, galangal, palm sugar, remaining coconut milk and 1 teaspoon salt. Cook over low heat for 15 minutes.

3 Add the tofu, bamboo shoots and chilli. Simmer for a further 3–5 minutes. Return to medium heat, add the seafood and lime juice and cook for a further 3 minutes, or until the seafood is just cooked. Remove from the heat.

4 Serve with steamed rice and garnish with the spring onion and coriander leaves.

SOY PASTA BAKE WITH PROSCIUTTO AND VEGETABLES

SERVES 6–8

Italian for ham, prosciutto, in English, specifically refers to smoked spiced Italian ham which is sliced very thinly and eaten raw. To make this a vegetarian dish, simply omit the prosciutto.

Preparation time: 25 minutes
Total cooking time: 1 hour

3 tablespoons olive oil
1/3 cup (35 g) dried breadcrumbs
250 g soy pasta
6 thin slices prosciutto, chopped
1 red onion, chopped
1 red capsicum, chopped
1/2 cup (100 g) semi-dried tomatoes,
   roughly chopped
3 tablespoons shredded fresh basil
1 cup (100 g) grated fresh Parmesan
4 eggs, lightly beaten
1 cup (250 ml) soy milk

1 Preheat the oven to moderate 180°C (350°F/Gas 4). Grease a 25 cm round ovenproof ceramic dish with a little of the oil, then coat the base and side with 2 tablespoons of the breadcrumbs. Cook the pasta in a large saucepan of boiling water until *al dente*. Drain and transfer to a large bowl.

2 Heat 1 tablespoon of the remaining oil in a large frying pan. Add the prosciutto and onion and cook over medium heat for 4–5 minutes, or until soft and golden. Add the capsicum and tomato and cook for 1–2 minutes. Toss into the pasta with the basil and Parmesan. Spoon into the dish.

3 Whisk the eggs and milk together and season, then pour over the pasta. Toss together the remaining breadcrumbs, the remaining oil and season. Sprinkle over the pasta. Bake for 40 minutes, or until set. Allow to stand for 5 minutes, then cut into wedges. Serve with a green salad, if desired.

SOY PASTA CARBONARA

SERVES 4

The term 'carbonara' is said to come from the Carbonari—a nineteenth century secret society working to unify Italy—who disguised themselves as "charcoal-burners" after being driven into hiding.

Preparation time: 10 minutes
Total cooking time: 20 minutes

6 rashers rindless bacon
2 eggs
1 egg yolk
1/2 cup (125 ml) creamy soy milk
2 cloves garlic, crushed
3/4 cup (75 g) grated fresh Parmesan
375 g soy pasta
30 g soy butter
1 tablespoon finely chopped fresh
   flat-leaf parsley

1 Cut the bacon into thin strips. Heat a frying pan, add the bacon and cook over low heat for 5 minutes, or until softened. Increase to medium and cook until thin and crispy. Remove the bacon and drain on paper towels. Place the eggs, egg yolk, soy milk, garlic and Parmesan in a bowl and mix well. Add the bacon.

2 Cook the soy pasta in a saucepan of boiling water until *al dente*. Drain and return to the pan. Add the soy butter and warm through. Turn off the heat, then add the egg mixture and the parsley and toss well—the heat of the pasta will cook the sauce. Serve with extra grated Parmesan, if desired.

SOY PASTA BAKE WITH PROSCIUTTO AND VEGETABLES

CHILLI CON CARNE WITH SOY BEANS

SERVES 4

Originally a Spanish dish simply meaning "chilli with meat", it has become one of the most popular dishes in Tex-Mex cuisine. Here we have replaced kidney beans with soy beans for a new flavour.

Preparation time: 15 minutes
Total cooking time: 1 hour 25 minutes

1 tablespoon soy bean oil
2 onions, chopped
2 cloves garlic, crushed
650 g beef mince
1 teaspoon paprika
1/2 teaspoon ground cumin
1 1/2 teaspoons chilli powder
415 g can chopped tomatoes
2 tablespoons tomato paste
2 tablespoons polenta
1 1/2 cups (375 ml) beef stock
420 g can soy beans, rinsed
   and drained
1/3 cup (20 g) chopped fresh parsley

1 Heat the oil in a heavy-based 2.5 litre flameproof casserole dish. Add the onion and garlic and cook over medium heat for 5 minutes, or until softened. Increase the heat to high and add the mince. Cook, stirring, for 3–4 minutes, or until the mince changes colour, breaking up any lumps with a wooden spoon.

2 Reduce the heat to medium, add the paprika, ground cumin, chilli powder, 1/2 teaspoon salt and 1/2 teaspoon freshly ground black pepper. Cook, stirring, for a further 1 minute. Stir in the chopped tomato, tomato paste, polenta and stock and bring to the boil. Reduce the heat and simmer, partially covered, for 1 hour. Stir in the soy beans and cook, covered, for a further 10 minutes. Garnish with the chopped parsley and serve with rice and corn chips.

TEMPURA WITH DIPPING SAUCE

SERVES 4

Tempura is said to have originated from Portuguese missionaries in Japan. They deep-fried fish and vegetables on days when meat was not eaten to make them more palatable.

Preparation time: 45 minutes
Total cooking time: 20 minutes

8 cap mushrooms
1 green capsicum
1 sheet dried nori
12 green beans, cut in half
300 g silken firm tofu, cut into
    2 cm cubes
1 small (400 g) eggplant
8 large raw prawns, peeled and
    deveined, tails intact
vegetable oil, for deep-frying
2/3 cup (80 g) soy flour
1 1/3 cup (165 g) plain flour
475 ml chilled soda water
2 egg yolks, lightly beaten
3 tablespoons plain flour, extra,
    for dusting
100 g daikon radish, peeled and
    finely shredded
2 tablespoons grated fresh ginger

DIPPING SAUCE
300 ml dashi
1/3 cup (80 ml) soy sauce
1/3 cup (80 ml) mirin

1   Wipe the mushroom caps clean and trim the stalks. Cut the capsicum into strips, then trim the end off the strips to form flat even-sized batons. Cut a narrow strip of nori and tie the beans together in groups of three, wetting the end of the nori to seal it. Pat the tofu dry with paper towels. Thinly slice the eggplant lengthways, then in half crossways. Place the prepared vegetables and prawns on a tray.

2   Fill a deep heavy-based saucepan one third full of oil and heat to 170°C (325°F), or until a cube of bread browns in 20 seconds.

3   Place the soy and plain flours in a large bowl and make a well in the centre. Pour in the soda water and egg yolk and loosely mix together with chopsticks or a fork until just combined—the batter should be quite thick and lumpy.

4   Coat the prawns, tofu and vegetables in the extra plain flour. Dip in the batter then deep-fry in batches, turning occasionally, for 1–3 minutes, or until crisp and golden and cooked through—do not overcrowd the pan. Remove with a slotted spoon and drain on paper towels. Between batches, skim off the bits of batter floating in the oil.

5   To make the dipping sauce, combine the dashi, soy sauce and mirin in a small saucepan. Bring to the boil then turn off the heat. Serve with the vegetable and prawn tempura and small mounds of daikon and ginger.

HEARTY SOY BEAN SOUP WITH POLENTA STICKS

SERVES 4

If you have any leftover polenta sticks, place them on a baking tray and heat in a moderate oven for 6 minutes. They are delicious eaten as a tasty snack on their own.

Preparation time: 20 minutes + overnight soaking + 1 hour chilling
Total cooking time: 3 hours 10 minutes

1/2 cup (120 g) dried soy beans
11/2 tablespoons soy bean oil
1 onion, finely chopped
4 rashers bacon, diced
800 g tomatoes, peeled and
    chopped (if using canned
    tomatoes, do not drain)
1 sprig basil, whole
3 cups (750 ml) chicken stock
fresh basil, extra, chopped,
    to garnish

POLENTA STICKS
11/2 cups (375 ml) soy milk
1/2 cup (75 g) polenta
1/4 cup (25 g) freshly grated
    Parmesan
1 teaspoon finely chopped fresh
    rosemary
30 g soy spread
1/4 cup (30 g) plain flour
soy oil, for deep-frying

1 Soak the soy beans in a large bowl with plenty of cold water for at least 8 hours or overnight. Rinse well. Transfer to a saucepan, cover with cold water and simmer for 2 hours, or until tender. Drain.

2 Heat the oil in a saucepan. Add the onion and bacon and cook for 5 minutes, or until soft. Add the tomato and cook for 5 minutes, or until pulpy. Stir in the basil, stock and 1 cup (250 ml) water. Bring to the boil, reduce the heat and simmer for 20 minutes. Add the beans and heat through.

3 To make the polenta sticks, place the soy milk and 11/2 cups (375 ml) water in a saucepan. Bring to the boil over high heat and add 1/2 teaspoon salt. Reduce the heat to low and add the polenta in a steady stream, whisking constantly to prevent lumps. Simmer, stirring with a wooden spoon, for 20–25 minutes, or until it pulls away from the side of the pan. Add the Parmesan, rosemary and soy spread and mix well. Season to taste.

4 Grease a 12 x 22 cm loaf tin. Spoon the polenta into the tin and smooth the surface with a wet spatula. Chill in the refrigerator for at least 1 hour (preferably overnight), or until set. Cut the polenta into 24 sticks (1.5 x 9 cm) and lightly coat in plain flour. Fill a heavy-based saucepan one third full with the soy oil and heat to 170°C (325°F), or until a cube of bread browns in 20 seconds. Deep-fry in batches for 2 minutes, or until golden brown all over—turn with tongs. Drain well. Spoon the soup into bowls and season to taste. Garnish with extra basil and serve with the polenta sticks.

CHINESE BEEF IN SOY

SERVES 4

Table salt seldom makes an appearance in Asian cooking because the sodium-rich soy sauce is used for flavouring instead.

Preparation time: 20 minutes +
    overnight marinating
Total cooking time: 1 hour 45 minutes

700 g chuck steak, trimmed and
    cut into 2 cm cubes
1/3 cup (80 ml) dark soy sauce
2 tablespoons honey
1 tablespoon wine vinegar
3 tablespoons soy bean oil
4 cloves garlic, chopped
8 spring onions, finely sliced
1 tablespoon grated fresh ginger
2 star anise
1/2 teaspoon ground cloves
1 1/2 cups (375 ml) beef stock
1/2 cup (125 ml) red wine
spring onions, extra, sliced,
    to garnish

1 Place the meat in a non-metallic dish. Combine the soy sauce, honey and vinegar in a small bowl, then pour over the meat. Cover with plastic wrap and marinate for at least 2 hours, or preferably overnight. Drain, reserving the marinade, and pat the cubes dry.

2 Place 1 tablespoon of the oil in a saucepan and brown the meat in three batches, for 3–4 minutes per batch—add another tablespoon of oil, if necessary. Remove the meat. Add the remaining oil and fry the garlic, spring onion, ginger, star anise and cloves for 1–2 minutes, or until fragrant.

3 Return all the meat to the pan, add the reserved marinade, stock and wine. Bring to the boil and simmer, covered, for 1 hour 15 minutes. Cook, uncovered, for a further 15 minutes, or until the sauce is syrupy and the meat is tender.

4 Garnish with the extra sliced spring onions and serve immediately with steamed rice.

SPICY NOODLES WITH PORK AND TOFU

SERVES 4

Due to their thickness, Hokkien noodles take on a lot of sauce and therefore flavour, making them the best noodles for any saucy stir-fry.

Preparation time: 20 minutes
Total cooking time: 15 minutes

250 g Hokkien noodles
1 tablespoon oil
500 g pork fillet, thinly sliced
2 cloves garlic, crushed
2 cm x 2 cm piece fresh ginger,
    julienned
100 g snow peas, sliced
100 g fresh shiitake mushrooms,
    sliced
1/2 teaspoon five-spice powder
2 tablespoons hoisin sauce
2 tablespoons soy sauce
1/4 cup (60 ml) vegetable stock
200 g fried tofu puffs, sliced
100 g soy bean sprouts
fried red Asian shallot flakes,
    to garnish

1   Cook the noodles in a large saucepan of boiling water for 2–3 minutes, or until tender. Drain.

2   Heat a wok over high heat, add half the oil and swirl to coat. Add the pork in two batches and stir-fry for 2 minutes each batch, or until browned. Remove from the wok.

3   Add a little more oil if necessary, then add the garlic and ginger and stir-fry for 30 seconds, or until fragrant. Add the snow peas, mushrooms and five-spice powder and cook for a further 1 minute. Pour in the hoisin sauce, soy sauce and stock and cook, stirring constantly, for 1–2 minutes. Add the tofu, soy bean sprouts, noodles and pork and toss to warm through. Serve immediately, garnished with the fried shallot flakes.

TUNA STEAKS AND SOY BEAN SALAD

SERVES 4

Tuna are a warm-blooded ocean fish with a pink-red, coarse-grained flesh. Eaten raw or grilled, the rich flavour is very popular and is commonly available in steaks.

Preparation time: 35 minutes
Total cooking time: 10 minutes

GINGER DRESSING
1/4 cup (60 ml) soy bean oil
2 tablespoons white wine vinegar
1 tablespoon grated fresh ginger
2 teaspoons honey
2 teaspoons salt-reduced soy sauce

2 carrots, sliced on the diagonal
2 zucchini, sliced on the diagonal
1 red capsicum, cut into 2 cm cubes
4 tuna steaks (about 180 g each),
    cut into cubes
soy bean oil, for brushing
1/2 small red onion, cut into thin
    wedges
150 g cherry tomatoes, halved
300 g can soy beans, rinsed and
    drained
1 tablespoon baby capers
125 g baby rocket leaves

1 To make the ginger dressing, place the oil, vinegar, ginger, honey and soy sauce in a jar and shake well.

2 Bring a saucepan of water to the boil. Add the carrot, zucchini and capsicum and cook, covered, for 1 minute. Drain and cool quickly under cold running water. Drain well.

3 Pat the tuna cubes dry with paper towels, then brush lightly with a little oil. Cook on a hot chargrill or barbecue plate for 1–2 minutes each side, or until cooked to your liking—the centre should still be pink.

4 Place the blanched vegetables, onion, tomato, soy beans, capers and rocket in a large bowl. Add the dressing and toss together. Divide among four serving bowls and toss in the cubes of tuna. Serve immediately.

SOY BEAN CASSEROLE WITH PORK SAUSAGES

SERVES 4

For a little more flavour, try one of the many varieties of thin sausages with extra spices available from your butcher or local supermarket. Serve this satisfying casserole with fresh crusty bread.

Preparation time: 25 minutes +
    overnight soaking
Total cooking time: 4 hours

1½ cups (300 g) dried soy beans
8 thin pork sausages (575 g)
2 tablespoons soy bean oil
1 red onion, chopped
4 cloves garlic, chopped
1 large carrot, diced
1 celery stick, diced
2 x 415 g cans chopped tomatoes
1 tablespoon tomato paste
1 cup (250 ml) white wine
2 sprigs fresh thyme
1 teaspoon dried oregano leaves
1 tablespoon fresh oregano,
    chopped

1 Soak the soy beans in a large bowl of cold water for at least 8 hours, or overnight. Drain well. Place in a large saucepan with enough fresh water to cover. Bring to the boil, then reduce the heat and slowly simmer for 1 hour 15 minutes to 2 hours—keep the beans covered with water during cooking. Drain well.

2 Prick the sausages all over. Heat a frying pan and cook, turning, for 10 minutes, or until browned all over. Drain on paper towels.

3 Heat the oil in a 3.5 litre flameproof casserole dish. Add the onion and garlic and cook on the stove top over medium heat for 3–5 minutes, or until softened. Add the carrot and celery. Cook, stirring, for a further 5 minutes. Stir in the tomato, paste, wine, thyme and dried oregano and bring to the boil. Reduce the heat and simmer, stirring often, for 10 minutes, or until the liquid has reduced and thickened slightly.

4 Preheat the oven to warm 160°C (315°F/Gas 2–3). Add the sausages, beans and 1 cup (250 ml) water to the casserole dish. Bake, covered, for 2 hours. Stir occasionally, adding more water if necessary to keep the beans just covered.

5 Return the casserole dish to the stove top, skim off any fat, then stir over medium heat until the liquid has reduced and thickened slightly. Remove the thyme sprigs and stir in the fresh oregano.

PHAD THAI WITH TOFU, CHICKEN AND PRAWNS

SERVES 4

Although similar to dried rice vermicelli, rice stick noodles are broader and thicker and are the centrepiece of this very popular Thai noodle dish.

Preparation time: 25 minutes +
    10 minutes soaking
Total cooking time: 10 minutes

250 g dried wide rice stick noodles
2 tablespoons soy bean oil
3 cloves garlic, finely chopped
2 small fresh red chillies, seeded
    and chopped
150 g chicken breast fillet,
    thinly sliced
200 g raw prawns, peeled and
    deveined, tails intact
100 g fried tofu puffs, julienned
3 tablespoons fish sauce
3 tablespoons lime juice
3 teaspoons palm or soft brown
    sugar
1 cup (90 g) soy bean sprouts,
    trimmed
¼ cup (40 g) unsalted roasted
    peanuts, chopped
3 tablespoons fresh coriander leaves
lime wedges, to garnish

1 Soak the noodles in warm water for 10 minutes, or until soft. Drain.

2 Heat a large wok or frying pan until hot, add the oil and swirl to coat. Add the garlic, chilli and chicken and stir-fry for 2 minutes. Stir in the prawns and cook for a further 2 minutes. Toss in the noodles and tofu until heated.

3 Add the fish sauce, lime juice and sugar and gently toss until well combined and heated through.

4 Spoon onto a platter and sprinkle with the sprouts, peanuts and coriander. Garnish with lime wedges.

SALMON WITH MISO AND SOY NOODLES

SERVES 6

This noodle dish is a great light meal in summer, suitable for outdoor entertaining—make the noodle salad and dressing, then chargrill the salmon on the barbecue just before serving.

Preparation time: 20 minutes
Total cooking time: 15 minutes

300 g soba noodles
1 tablespoon soy bean oil
3 teaspoons white miso paste
100 ml honey
1½ tablespoons sesame oil
6 salmon fillets, boned and
   skin removed
1 teaspoon chopped garlic
1 tablespoon grated fresh ginger
1 carrot, julienned
6 small spring onions, thinly sliced
1 cup (70 g) soy bean sprouts
⅓ cup (80 ml) rice vinegar
3 tablespoons light soy sauce
1 teaspoon sesame oil, extra
1 tablespoon toasted sesame seeds
mustard cress, to garnish

1 Preheat the oven to moderate 180°C (350°F/Gas 4). Fill a large saucepan three quarters full with water and bring to the boil. Add the soba noodles and return to the boil. Cook for 1 minute, then add 1 cup (250 ml) cold water. Boil for 1–2 minutes, then add another 1 cup (250 ml) water. Boil for 2 minutes, or until tender, then drain and toss with ½ teaspoon of the soy bean oil.

2 Combine the miso, honey, sesame oil and 1 tablespoon water to form a paste. Brush over the salmon, then sear on a hot chargrill for 30 seconds on each side. Brush the salmon with the remaining paste and place on a baking tray. Bake for 6 minutes, then cover and rest in a warm place.

3 Heat the remaining soy oil in a wok. Add the garlic, ginger, carrot, spring onion and sprouts, and stir-fry for 1 minute—the vegetables should not brown, but remain crisp and bright. Add the noodles, rice vinegar, soy sauce and extra sesame oil and stir-fry quickly to heat through.

4 Divide the noodles among six serving plates, top with a portion of salmon and sprinkle with the sesame seeds. Garnish with the mustard cress.

MA PO TOFU WITH BEEF MINCE

SERVES 4–6

There are two types of fermented black beans, but this recipe refers to the soy bean variety. Although soy beans are commonly light in colour, they darken during the fermenting process.

Preparation time: 15 minutes +
   5 minutes soaking
Total cooking time: 10 minutes

2 tablespoons fermented
   black beans
2 tablespoons vegetable oil
200 g minced beef
1 tablespoon finely chopped fresh
   ginger
3 spring onions, finely chopped
1/2 cup (125 ml) vegetable stock
2 tablespoons soy sauce
1 tablespoon chilli bean paste
2 tablespoons Chinese rice wine
450 g firm tofu
2 cloves garlic, coarsely chopped
1 tablespoon cornflour
2 teaspoons sesame oil

1 Place the black beans in a bowl of cold water and soak for 5 minutes. Drain and finely chop.

2 Heat the oil in a wok or non-stick frying pan. Add the mince and season with salt and pepper. Stir-fry over high heat for 2 minutes, or until the meat changes colour—use a wooden spoon to break up any lumps. Add the black beans, ginger and spring onion and stir-fry for a further 2 minutes.

3 Stir in the vegetable stock, soy sauce, chilli bean paste and rice wine. Cut the tofu into 1.5 cm cubes, add to the wok with the garlic, and stir gently until the tofu is well coated. Cook over low heat for a further 3 minutes.

4 Combine the cornflour with 3 tablespoons water until it forms a smooth paste. Add to the wok with the sesame oil. Stir over medium heat for 1 minute, or until thickened slightly. Serve immediately with boiled rice.

SOY BEAN MOUSSAKA

SERVES 4–6

'Moussaka' comes from the Arabic word musaqqâ which means 'moistened', which refers to the tomato juices. Although the Arabic spelling is used, this traditional dish is actually from Turkey.

Preparation time: 30 minutes
Total cooking time: 1 hour 20 minutes

500 g eggplant, cut into 1 cm slices
soy bean oil, for brushing
2 tablespoons soy bean oil, extra
1 large onion, chopped
2 cloves garlic, chopped
650 g minced lamb
2 tablespoons tomato paste
415 g can chopped tomatoes
1 cup (250 ml) white wine or water
1 teaspoon ground cinnamon
1/3 cup (20 g) chopped fresh
    parsley
1 teaspoon chopped fresh oregano
300 g can soy beans, rinsed and
    drained

CHEESE SAUCE
75 g soy spread or margarine
1/3 cup (40 g) plain flour
2 1/2 cups (625 ml) soy milk
1/2 cup (60 g) grated Cheddar
1/2 teaspoon ground nutmeg
1 egg

1 Brush the eggplant slices with soy bean oil. Chargrill, or grill under a hot grill, for 2–3 minutes on each side, or until golden brown and softened. Keep warm.

2 Heat the extra soy bean oil in a frying pan. Add the onion and garlic and cook over medium heat for 5 minutes, or until softened. Increase the heat and add the mince. Cook, stirring, for 5 minutes, or until the mince changes colour—use a wooden spoon to break up any lumps.

3 Reduce the heat and add the tomato paste, tomatoes, wine, cinnamon, parsley and oregano. Simmer for 15 minutes, or until the liquid has been absorbed. Season well with salt and pepper, then stir in the beans. Preheat the oven to moderate 180°C (350°F/Gas 4).

4 To make the cheese sauce, heat the soy spread in a saucepan. Stir in the flour and cook, stirring, for 1 minute. Remove from the heat and whisk in the soy milk. Return to the heat and stir constantly until thickened. Cook for a further 2 minutes, then remove from the heat and stir in the cheese and nutmeg. Season well with salt and ground black pepper. Leave for 5 minutes then whisk in the egg.

5 Spoon one third of the meat and bean mixture on the base of a 1.5 litre casserole dish and arrange one third of the eggplant slices on top. Layer twice more ending with the eggplant slices, pressing down firmly and evenly with the back of a spoon. Pour the sauce over the eggplant and bake for 50 minutes, or until the top is set and golden brown. Serve hot.

TERIYAKI BEEF STIR-FRY WITH SOY BEANS

SERVES 4

'Teriyaki' is a Japanese meat dish that is marinated in soy sauce and rice wine. The term is a combination of 'teri' meaning gloss or shine, and 'yaki' meaning to grill or cook.

Preparation time: 15 minutes
Total cooking time: 20 minutes

400 g frozen soy beans
1 tablespoon peanut oil
700 g centre cut rump steak,
    cut into 1 cm x 5 cm strips
6 spring onions, finely sliced
2 cloves garlic, chopped
2 teaspoons finely chopped fresh
    ginger
50 g soy bean sprouts
1 red capsicum, finely sliced
1 tablespoon mirin
2 tablespoons sake
2 tablespoons Japanese soy sauce
2 teaspoons sugar

1 Cook the soy beans in a saucepan of boiling water for 2 minutes. Drain.

2 Heat a large wok until very hot. Add 2 teaspoons of the peanut oil and swirl to coat the side. Cook the beef in three batches for 3–4 minutes per batch, or until well browned. Remove from the wok and keep warm. Add the spring onion and stir-fry for 30 seconds, or until wilted.

3 Return the beef to the wok, add the garlic, ginger, soy beans, soy bean sprouts and capsicum, and stir-fry for 2 minutes. Combine the mirin, sake, Japanese soy sauce and sugar. Add the sauce to the wok and stir-fry until heated through. Serve hot with steamed rice.

TERIYAKI CHICKEN AND SOY BEAN STIR-FRY

This recipe is a variation of the Teriyaki beef stir-fry with soy beans—like the above dish, it serves 4 and requires the same preparation and cooking times.

375 g frozen soy beans
2 tablespoons flour
1/4 teaspoon five-spice powder
700 g chicken breast fillet
3 tablespoons peanut oil
6 spring onions, finely sliced
2 cloves garlic, chopped
2 teaspoons finely chopped fresh
    ginger
50 g soy bean sprouts
1 red capsicum, finely sliced
1 tablespoon mirin
2 tablespoons sake
2 tablespoons Japanese soy sauce
2 teaspoons sugar

1 Cook the soy beans in a saucepan of boiling water for 2 minutes. Drain.

2 Combine the flour and the five-spice powder. Cut the chicken into thin strips, then dust in the seasoned flour. Shake off the excess flour.

3 Heat a large wok until very hot. Add the peanut oil and swirl to coat. Cook the chicken in batches for 2 minutes, or until golden. Remove from the wok and keep warm. Add the spring onion to the wok and stir-fry for 30 seconds, or until wilted.

4 Return the chicken to the wok, add the garlic, ginger, soy bean sprouts, capsicum and the soy beans and stir-fry for 2 minutes. Combine the mirin, sake, Japanese soy sauce and sugar. Add the sauce to the wok and stir-fry until heated through. Serve hot with steamed rice.

TERIYAKI BEEF STIR-FRY WITH SOY BEANS

Clockwise from bottom left:
Fresh soy bean nibblies, Soy bean
dip with soy and linseed crostini,
Bean curd sushi (inari sushi), and
Crispy tofu prawn balls.

SOY FOR PARTIES

Clockwise from bottom left:
Sesame-crusted tofu snacks,
Avocado and black bean salsa,
Soy bean hummus, purchased soy
chips, Crunchy spiced soy beans,
and Spicy tempeh sticks.

SOY FOR PARTIES

Watch your guests mingle, discussing the weather and politics, and carrying napkins laden with these nibblies. When the napkin is empty and there's a pause in conversation they'll be back for more.

SOY BEAN DIP WITH SOY AND LINSEED CROSTINI

Cook 200 g frozen soy beans in 2 cups (500 ml) vegetable stock for 10–12 minutes. Drain, reserving 1/4 cup (60 ml) of the stock. Mix the beans in a food processor with 1 clove crushed garlic, 1/2 cup (30 g) chopped fresh basil, 1 tablespoon extra virgin olive oil and the reserved stock, occasionally scraping down the sides, until smooth. Serve warm with soy and linseed bread crostini. Makes 1 1/2 cups. To make the crostini, preheat the oven to moderate 180°C (350°F/Gas 4). Remove the crusts from 6 slices soy and linseed bread. Cut each slice into 2.5 cm wide fingers. Place on an oven tray and bake for 8 minutes, or until golden. Rub with the cut side of 1/2 clove garlic and serve warm with the soy bean dip.

CRISPY TOFU PRAWN BALLS

Peel and devein 400 g raw prawns and place in a blender with 200 g silken firm tofu, 1/2 tablespoon grated fresh ginger, 1 tablespoon fish sauce, 1/2 cup (15 g) coriander leaves and 3 chopped small fresh red chillies and blend together well. Transfer to a bowl and stir in 1/2 cup (40 g) soy flour. Chill for 30 minutes. To make the dipping sauce, combine 1 tablespoon fish sauce, 1 tablespoon rice vinegar, 1 tablespoon lime juice, 1 tablespoon water, 1/2 teaspoon sugar and 1 tablespoon chopped fresh coriander leaves and whisk together well. Fill a deep, heavy-based saucepan one third full of oil and heat to 170°C (325°F), or until a cube of bread browns in 20 seconds. Add rounded teaspoons of the prawn mixture and cook in batches for 3 minutes, or until browned all over. Drain on paper towels. Serve with the dipping sauce. Makes about 25.

FRESH SOY BEAN NIBBLIES

Wash 350 g frozen soy beans in pods. Fill a large saucepan with water, add 2 teaspoons salt and 1 cm x 10 cm piece dried kombu, then bring to the boil. Add the soy beans and cook for 5 minutes. Drain and cool. Serve the pods seasoned with a little sea salt.

BEAN CURD SUSHI (INARI SUSHI)

Wash 1¼ cups (275 g) short-grain rice several times until the water runs clear. Drain. Soak the rice in a saucepan with 400 ml water for 30 minutes. Add a pinch of salt and cover with a tea towel stretched under a tight-fitting lid. Bring to the boil, then reduce to very low and simmer for 10 minutes. Remove from the heat and leave, covered, for 15 minutes. Soak 4 large dried shiitake mushrooms in 1½ cups (375 ml) warm water for 30 minutes. Drain, reserving the mushroom liquid. Trim the stems and thinly slice the caps. Place 2½ tablespoons rice vinegar, 1 tablespoon mirin, 2 tablespoons sugar and 1½ teaspoons salt in a small saucepan. Stir over low heat for 2 minutes, or until the sugar has dissolved. Cool to room temperature and stir in ¼ teaspoon sesame oil. Place the rice in a large bowl and sprinkle one third of the vinegar mixture over the top, then quickly and lightly fold in with a large metal spoon. Repeat until all the vinegar mixture is used. Gently fold in the mushrooms. Cut a slit along one edge of 12 pre-cooked seasoned bean curd sheets (inari) then gently ease the sheets apart to make a pouch. Moisten your hands with a little of the reserved mushroom liquid, take a handful of rice, shape it into an oval and gently press it inside the bean curd sheets, leaving 1 cm at the top. Fold over the edges like an envelope. Repeat with the remaining sheets and rice. To serve, place cut-side-down on a plate and sprinkle with 2 teaspoons lightly toasted sesame seeds.

CRUNCHY SPICED SOY BEANS

Soak 100 g dried soy beans in plenty of water overnight. Drain, then dry on paper towels. Heat 1 cm sunflower oil in a deep frying pan. Add the beans and cook for 10–12 minutes, or until medium brown and crisp. Drain on paper towels. Cool. Heat a clean frying pan over medium heat. Add 1 tablespoon sesame seeds and 1 teaspoon sea salt and lightly toast for 2–4 minutes, stirring continually. Grind the sesame seed mixture in a spice grinder until fine. Combine the beans and the sesame salt. Store in an airtight container for 3 weeks.

SOY BEAN HUMMUS

Soak 125 g dried soy beans in plenty of water overnight. Drain and cook in a large saucepan of boiling water for 1½–2 hours, or until tender. Drain. Heat 1 tablespoon soy bean oil in a frying pan and cook 1 small finely chopped onion over medium heat for 5–8 minutes, or until soft. Add 1½ teaspoons ground cumin and a pinch of cayenne pepper and cook over high heat for 1 minute, or until aromatic. Stir in the soy beans to coat. Place the mixture in a food processor with 2 tablespoons lemon juice, ½ cup (125 ml) olive oil, 2 crushed cloves garlic. Season with salt and process until smooth—add a little water for a thinner consistency. Makes about 2 cups (500 ml). Can be made up to 5 days ahead and stored in an airtight container in the fridge.

SESAME-CRUSTED TOFU SNACKS

Cut 300 g tofu into 2 cm cubes. Place 1½ tablespoons white sesame seeds, 1½ tablespoons black sesame seeds, 2 tablespoons cornflour on a plate and season. Gently toss the tofu in the sesame seed mixture to coat. Heat 2 tablespoons soy bean oil in a large, heavy-based frying pan. Add the tofu in batches and fry over medium heat, turning frequently, for 3–4 minutes, or until toasted on all sides—add a little more oil if necessary. Drain on paper towels. To make the dipping sauce, combine 2 tablespoons light soy sauce, 2 tablespoons mirin and 1 tablespoon finely chopped fresh ginger. Serve with the tofu cubes.

AVOCADO AND BLACK BEAN SALSA

Rinse and drain 100 g canned black soy beans, then place in a bowl with 1 chopped, seeded and diced red capsicum, 1 diced avocado, 1/2 small diced red onion, 1 cup (50 g) coriander leaves, finely chopped, 1 finely chopped small fresh red chilli, 2 tablespoons lime juice and salt and pepper. Gently toss to combine, then leave for 10 minutes for the flavours to infuse. Serve with purchased soy chips.

SPICY TEMPEH STICKS

Place 3 cloves coarsley chopped garlic, 4 chopped spring onions, 4 chopped blanched almonds and 1/4 cup (60 ml) water in a blender and process until almost smooth. Add 1 tablespoon ground coriander, 1 teaspoon salt, 1/4 teaspoon pepper and 1/4 teaspoon cayenne pepper and briefly blend to combine. Transfer to a large bowl, then whisk in 1 tablespoon plain flour. Cut a 300 g block seasoned tempeh lengthways into 6 x 2 cm strips, then cut in half lengthways to form large French fry shapes. Fill a deep, heavy-based saucepan one third full of oil and heat to moderate 180°C (350°F), or until a cube of bread browns in 15 seconds. Coat the tempeh in the seasoning and fry in batches for 3–4 minutes, or until golden brown and crisp. Remove with a slotted spoon and drain on paper towels. Repeat with the remaining tempeh. Serve while still hot and crisp.

SOY FOR DESSERT

Have you noticed that no matter how full you are, you always have room for dessert? A sweet end to a special meal, or an unabashed need for a little self-pampering, however you justify it, there is no doubt that dessert is an indulgence—it's a reward for completing the main course successfully. Creamy, crunchy, baked, frozen, hot, cold, classic and new—all of these favourite desserts contain soy in some form.

CHOCOLATE MOUSSE

SERVES 4

Brandy can be replaced with a different flavoured liqueur (such as coffee, almond or hazelnut). For added texture and flavour, stir in a couple of tablespoons of finely chopped toasted nuts before setting.

Preparation time: 25 minutes +
    3 hours chilling
Total cooking time: Nil

100 g good-quality dark
    chocolate
1 tablespoon brandy
200 g silken tofu
3 eggs, separated
1 tablespoon caster sugar
cream or soy yoghurt, to serve
dark chocolate, extra, grated,
    to garnish

1 Roughly chop the chocolate and melt in a heatproof bowl over a saucepan of simmering water—do not let the base of the bowl touch the water. Remove the bowl from the heat and leave to cool slightly.

2 Combine the chocolate, brandy, tofu and egg yolks in a food processor. Transfer to a bowl.

3 Beat the egg whites until soft peaks form. Continue beating and gradually add the sugar. Thoroughly mix 1 tablespoon of the egg white mixture into the chocolate, then gently fold the rest through until well combined.

4 Divide the mixture among four 150 ml ramekins or individual serving bowls and refrigerate for 2–3 hours, or until set. Serve with cream or soy yoghurt and garnish with grated chocolate.

LEMON MOUSSE

SERVES 4

The simple delicious flavour of this mousse relies on a good-quality lemon butter. Any leftover butter can be spooned into mini pastry cases for a quick and easy dessert.

Preparation time: 15 minutes +
    1 hour chilling
Total cooking time: Nil

180 g jar good-quality lemon butter
200 g soy custard
2 egg whites

1 Place the lemon butter and soy custard in a bowl and gently stir together until well combined.

2 Beat the egg whites and a pinch of salt in a dry clean bowl with electric beaters until stiff peaks form.

3 Fold 2 tablespoons of the egg white into the lemon mixture with a metal spoon, then fold in the remaining egg whites. Spoon into four serving bowls and refrigerate for at least 1 hour.

CHOCOLATE MOUSSE

CARAMEL RICE PUDDING

SERVES 4

During the time of Charles I, the traditional rice pudding (rice cooked in milk with sugar and cinnamon) was considered an aphrodisiac.

Preparation time: 15 minutes
Total cooking time: 1 hour 15 minutes

½ cup (120 g) medium-grain or
   short-grain rice
2 eggs
2 tablespoons soft brown sugar
1½ cups (375 ml) vanilla-flavoured
   soy milk
2 tablespoons caramel topping
½ cup (125 ml) cream
½ teaspoon ground nutmeg
ground nutmeg, extra, to garnish

1 Preheat the oven to warm 160°C (315°F/Gas 2–3). Grease a 1.5 litre ovenproof ceramic dish. Cook the rice in a saucepan of boiling water for 12 minutes, or until just tender. Drain and cool slightly.

2 Place the eggs, brown sugar, soy milk, caramel topping and cream in a large bowl and whisk together well. Fold in the rice. Pour the mixture into the prepared dish and sprinkle the surface with the nutmeg. Place the ceramic dish in a deep baking tin and pour in enough boiling water to come halfway up the sides.

3 Bake for 30 minutes, then stir with a fork to distribute the rice evenly. Cook for a further 30 minutes, or until the custard is just set. Serve hot or warm. Sprinkle with the extra ground nutmeg just before serving.

FROZEN MANGO AND BANANA TERRINE

SERVES 6

Hindu legend has it that the banana was the forbidden fruit and that Adam and Eve used banana leaves to cover themselves instead of the widely accepted fig leaf.

Preparation time: 20 minutes +
    overnight freezing
Total cooking time: Nil

soy bean oil, for greasing
1 cup (90 g) shredded coconut
125 g silken tofu
1/2 cup (125 ml) soy milk
1/2 cup (125 ml) thick coconut
    cream
125 g macadamia spread
1/4 cup (90 g) honey
4 ripe lady finger bananas
2 mangoes, peeled and cut into
    1 cm cubes
1/2 cup (80 g) sultanas
1 teaspoon soy butter

1 Grease a 1.5 litre (8 x 8 x 22 cm) terrine dish with soy bean oil and line with baking paper. Sprinkle half the coconut over the base of the dish.

2 Blend the tofu, soy milk, coconut cream, macadamia spread, honey and bananas in a food processor until smooth.

3 Pour the tofu and banana mixture into the prepared dish and evenly spread the mango and sultanas on top—gently swirl with a knife to distribute evenly. Sprinkle the remaining coconut over the fruit. Cover with plastic wrap and freeze for 8 hours, or overnight.

4 Just before serving, uncover the terrine and place in a sink of hot water for 1 minute, ensuring the water doesn't reach the top of the tin. Wipe the tin with a tea towel, then run a knife around the edges and turn out onto a serving plate. Dip a sharp knife in hot water, slice and serve immediately.

SOY PANNA COTTA WITH ORANGE COMPOTE

SERVES 4

This Italian dessert is traditionally made with cream. Here it is reinvented using soy milk and a fruit-flavoured tofu product without compromising the dish's famous smooth, creamy texture.

Preparation time: 20 minutes +
    4 hours refrigeration
Total cooking time: 20 minutes

soy bean oil, for brushing
2 tablespoons caster sugar
1 cup (250 ml) creamy soy milk
1¼ gelatine leaves
150 g apricot tofu dessert
¼ teaspoon vanilla essence

ORANGE COMPOTE
2 oranges
¼ cup (60 g) caster sugar
1 cinnamon stick

1 Lightly grease four ¼ cup (60 ml) ramekins with the oil. Place the sugar and ²/₃ cup (170 ml) of the soy milk in a saucepan. Stir over medium heat until the sugar has dissolved, then bring to the boil. Remove from the heat and set aside.

2 Cover the gelatine leaves with water in a small bowl and leave for 5 minutes, or until soft. Squeeze out any excess water. Add to the soy milk mixture and stir until dissolved. Leave to cool slightly.

3 Blend the tofu dessert in a food processor until smooth, then transfer to a bowl. Whisk in the soy milk mixture, then the vanilla essence and the remaining soy milk. Pour the mixture through a fine sieve. Pour into the prepared ramekins and refrigerate for at least 4 hours, or until set.

4 To make the orange compote, peel and segment the oranges over a bowl, to the catch the excess juice—reserve ¼ cup (60 ml) of the juice. Place the sugar in a small saucepan with the reserved juice, cinnamon stick and ³/₄ cup (185 ml) water. Bring to the boil and stir until the sugar dissolves. Reduce the heat and simmer for 10–12 minutes, or until it thickens slightly. Remove from the heat and sit for 5 minutes. Pour the syrup over the orange segments and leave to cool.

5 Carefully turn the panna cotta onto serving plates. Spoon some orange segments around each one and drizzle with a little of the extra syrup.

DATE CUSTARD TART

SERVES 8

Dates are the fruit of the palm tree and can be traced to the hot, dry desert regions of North Africa, the Middle East and India.

Preparation time: 35 minutes + 20 minutes refrigeration
Total cooking time: 1 hour 40 minutes

1¼ cups (155 g) plain flour
80 g cold butter, chopped
60 g ground walnuts
2 tablespoons iced water
icing sugar, for dusting

FILLING
130 g fresh dates
1 cup (250 ml) soy milk
½ vanilla bean
2 eggs
¼ cup (60 g) caster sugar

1 Sift the flour into a large bowl and add the butter. Rub the butter into the flour with your fingertips until it resembles fine breadcrumbs. Stir in the walnuts, then make a well in the centre. Add the iced water and mix with a flat-bladed knife, using a cutting action until the mixture comes together in small beads.

2 Gently gather the dough together into a ball and transfer to a sheet of baking paper. Roll out to fit a 22 cm loose-bottomed fluted flan tin. Line the tin with the pastry, trim the edges and refrigerate for 20 minutes.

3 Preheat the oven to warm 170°C (325°F/Gas 3). Line the pastry shell with a sheet of baking paper large enough to cover the base and side of the tin and fill with baking beads or uncooked rice. Bake for 15 minutes, remove the paper and beads, then bake for a further 20 minutes, or until the pastry is lightly golden and dry. Cool.

4 To make the filling, cut the dates into quarters lengthways and discard the stones. Arrange, cut-side-down, in circles on the pastry base. Pour the soy milk into a saucepan. Split the vanilla bean lengthways, scrape the seeds into the milk and add the bean. Slowly heat the soy milk until almost boiling.

5 Meanwhile, whisk the eggs and sugar together in a bowl. Slowly pour the hot milk onto the egg mixture, whisking gently as you pour. Discard the vanilla bean.

6 Place the tin on a flat baking tray. Gently pour the custard over the dates. Bake for 1 hour, or until the custard has set. Cool to room temperature, then dust with icing sugar before serving.

COFFEE SOY ICE CREAM WITH AMARETTO SYRUP

COFFEE SOY ICE CREAM WITH AMARETTO SYRUP

SERVES 4

The ideal dessert to serve a coffee lover with a sweet-tooth—this ice cream is flavoured with coffee and covered in a sweet liqueur syrup.

Preparation time: 20 minutes +
    35 minutes cooling +
    9 hours 30 minutes freezing
Total cooking time: 25 minutes

1½ cups (375 ml) coffee-flavoured
    soy milk
1 cup (250 ml) cream
1 teaspoon instant coffee
4 egg yolks
⅓ cup (90 g) sugar
50 g toasted flaked almonds

AMARETTO SYRUP
⅓ cup (90 g) caster sugar
3 tablespoons Amaretto liqueur

1 Bring the soy milk and cream to a simmer over low heat. Remove from the heat and stir in the coffee until dissolved. Beat the egg yolks and sugar with electric beaters for 2–3 minutes, or until light and creamy. Gradually whisk in the soy milk mixture. Return to the pan, stirring constantly for 5 minutes, or until thick enough to coat the back of a spoon and a line is left when you run a finger down the spoon. Remove from the heat and cool. Pour into a shallow metal tray, cover and freeze for 1 hour 30 minutes, or until half frozen. Blend in a food processor for 15 seconds, or until smooth. Return to the tray and freeze for 8 hours. Remove 15 minutes before serving.

2 To make the syrup, dissolve the sugar in ½ cup (125 ml) water in a saucepan over low heat. Simmer for 8–10 minutes, or until syrupy. Remove from the heat and stir in the liqueur. Cool, then drizzle over the ice cream. Garnish with almonds and serve immediately.

HOT FUDGE SAUCE

MAKES 2 CUPS

The rich, dark unsweetened Dutch cocoa (which has bicarbonate of soda added to it) is considered the best of all cocoas used in cooking.

Preparation time: 10 minutes
Total cooking time: 10 minutes

180 g silken tofu
⅓ cup (40 g) good-quality Dutch
    cocoa powder
⅓ cup (80 ml) vanilla soy milk
1 cup (350 g) golden syrup
1 teaspoon vanilla essence
50 g soy chocolate
2 teaspoons brandy

1 Blend the tofu, cocoa, soy milk, golden syrup and vanilla in a food processor. Chop the soy chocolate into small even-sized pieces and place in a heatproof bowl with the brandy. Place over a saucepan of simmering water, stirring until the chocolate has melted—ensure the base of the bowl doesn't touch the water.

2 Add the tofu mixture to the chocolate mixture and whisk for 5–8 minutes, or until smooth and glossy. Serve warm over soy ice cream.

BAKED CUSTARDS WITH POACHED TAMARILLOS

SERVES 4

The tamarillo is a tropical fruit related to the tomato and kiwi fruit. They should be blanched and peeled before eating. Once peeled, add to fruit salads or, in this case, poach in a sweet syrup and serve.

Preparation time: 20 minutes
Total cooking time: 50 minutes

3 eggs
1/4 cup (60 g) caster sugar
1 teaspoon vanilla essence
2 cups (500 ml) soy milk,
    warmed
1 tablespoon soft brown sugar

POACHED TAMARILLOS
4 tamarillos
1½ cups (375 g) caster sugar
1 cinnamon stick
4 cloves

1 Preheat the oven to warm 170°C (325°F/Gas 3). Place four 1/2 cup (125 ml) ramekin dishes in a deep baking tray.

2 Beat the eggs, sugar and vanilla in a large bowl. Gradually whisk in the soy milk, then strain through a fine sieve. Pour the milk mixture into the prepared ramekins, then pour enough boiling water into the baking tray until it comes halfway up the side of the ramekins.

3 Bake for 25 minutes, or until the custard is set and a skewer comes out clean when inserted in the centre. Evenly sprinkle the brown sugar on top and place under a hot grill for 2–3 minutes, or until the sugar melts and caramelises.

4 Meanwhile, to make the poached tamarillos, place the tamarillos in a saucepan of boiling water and cook for 30 seconds. Drain, cool slightly and peel off the skin. Place the sugar, cinnamon, cloves and 3 cups (750 ml) water in the cleaned pan and stir over medium heat until the sugar has dissolved. Bring the syrup to the boil and cook for 3 minutes. Reduce the heat to a simmer, add the tamarillos and cook for 6–8 minutes. Turn off the heat and leave in the syrup to cool. Remove the fruit from the pan, then return the syrup to the heat. Boil for 5–10 minutes, or until thickened. Cool. Halve the tamarillos, leaving the stalk intact. Serve with hot or warmed syrup and the baked custard.

BREAD AND BUTTER PUDDING

SERVES 6–8

For a really luscious bread and butter pudding, try using slices of fruit brioche or roughly torn croissants instead of bread.

Preparation time: 20 minutes +
    10 minutes standing
Total cooking time: 50 minutes

10 slices soy and linseed bread
50 g soy butter
30 g sultanas
2 tablespoons orange marmalade,
    melted
3 eggs
3 cups (750 ml) vanilla-flavoured
    soy milk
1/3 cup (90 g) caster sugar
1/2 teaspoon ground cinnamon
1/2 teaspoon caster sugar, extra
icing sugar, for dusting

1 Preheat the oven to moderate 180°C (350°F/Gas 4). Grease a 2 litre (26 x 16 x 5 cm) ovenproof dish. Cut the crusts off the bread, then spread with soy butter. Cut each slice in half on the diagonal. Arrange half the bread slices in the prepared dish, buttered-side-up, then sprinkle with half the sultanas. Layer with the remaining slices and sprinkle with the remaining sultanas. Add 1 tablespoon warm water to the melted marmalade, then brush liberally over the surface.

2 Whisk the eggs, soy milk and sugar together, pour evenly over the bread and leave for 10 minutes. Combine the cinnamon and extra sugar and sprinkle over the pudding.

3 Place the ovenproof dish in a deep baking tin. Pour enough boiling water into the baking tin until it comes halfway up the sides. Bake for 50 minutes, or until the custard is set and a skewer comes out clean when inserted in the centre. Dust with icing sugar and serve.

MANGO AND PASSIONFRUIT
INDIVIDUAL TRIFLES

SERVES 4

Fresh passionfruit pulp may be used instead of canned for this recipe—use half a passionfruit per layer. Drizzle a little honey over the top of each layer to sweeten.

Preparation time: 20 minutes +
    soaking time
Total cooking time: 5 minutes

6 sponge finger biscuits
¼ cup (60 ml) vanilla-flavoured
    soy milk
2 mangoes, thinly sliced
170 g can passionfruit pulp in
    syrup
2 x 200 g tubs apricot soy yoghurt
1 tablespoon flaked almonds

1 Crumble the sponge finger biscuits into a small bowl. Pour the vanilla-flavoured soy milk over the biscuit crumbs and allow to soak up the liquid.

2 Spoon 2 tablespoons of the crumb mixture into each of four 300 ml glasses. Divide half the mango and passionfruit among the glasses, then top each with 2 tablespoons of the yoghurt. Repeat with the remaining crumbs, mango, passionfruit and yoghurt.

3 Spread the flaked almonds evenly onto the base of a dry fying pan. Toast gently over low heat, stirring occasionally, until golden.

4 To serve, sprinkle the individual trifles with the toasted almonds and chill until ready to serve.

CHOCOLATE TOFU CHEESECAKE

SERVES 10

The heavenly qualities of chocolate are accepted in the most scientific of circles, and rightly so—when translated, the botanical name of the cacao tree means 'food of the gods'.

Preparation time: 20 minutes +
   6 hours refrigeration
Total cooking time: Nil

200 g chocolate-flavoured
   biscuits
90 g butter, melted
1 tablespoon gelatine
600 g silken tofu, drained
250 g soy cream cheese
1/2 cup (125 g) caster sugar
2 teaspoons vanilla essence
250 g dark chocolate, melted
   and cooled
2 tablespoons shaved chocolate
250 g strawberries, cut into quarters,
   to serve

1 Lightly grease a 23 cm springform tin and line the base with non-stick baking paper.

2 Place the biscuits in a food processor and blend until finely crushed. Add the butter and process until combined. Spoon the biscuit mixture into the prepared tin and evenly smooth over the base with the back of a spoon. Refrigerate until required.

3 Meanwhile, sprinkle the gelatine evenly over 1/4 cup (60 ml) warm water in a small bowl. Leave until the gelatine is spongy—do not stir. Bring a small saucepan of water to the boil, remove from the heat and place the bowl in the pan. The water should come halfway up the side of the bowl. Stir the gelatine until clear and dissolved.

4 Place the tofu, soy cream cheese, sugar, essence, melted chocolate and gelatine in a food processor and blend until smooth. Spoon the filling into the prepared tin and refrigerate for 6 hours, or until set.

5 Garnish with the shaved chocolate and serve with a generous pile of quartered strawberries.

PEACH CRUMBLE

SERVES 4

Fruit crumbles, with their simple topping, were thought to have been developed during World War II. The topping is quick and easy to prepare, and is used instead of pastry.

Preparation time: 15 minutes
Total cooking time: 25 minutes

2 x 415 g cans sliced peaches,
    drained
1/2 cup (45 g) flaked almonds
1/3 cup (60 g) soft brown sugar
1/3 cup (35 g) rolled oats
1/2 teaspoon baking powder
1/2 cup (60 g) plain flour
1/3 cup (35 g) soy flour
1/2 teaspoon gluten flour
75 g soy butter, chopped
soy custard, to serve

1 Preheat the oven to moderate 180°C (350°F/Gas 4). Place the peach slices in a 15 x 24 cm ovenproof ceramic dish. Combine the almonds, brown sugar, oats and baking powder in a bowl.

2 Sift the flours into a bowl and add the chopped soy butter. Rub the butter into the flour with your fingertips until crumbly. Stir in the almond mixture and spoon evenly over the peaches. Bake for 25 minutes, or until lightly golden brown. Serve hot or warm with the soy custard.

APPLE AND RHUBARB CRUMBLE

SERVES 4

This dish is a popular variation to the above Peach crumble. Many of your favourite fruits (pears, plums, cherries) can be used in the base with the same crumble topping.

Preparation time: 20 minutes
Total cooking time: 40 minutes

125 g soy butter
800 g Granny Smith apples, peeled
    and chopped
450 g rhubarb, cut unto 4 cm pieces
1 1/2 teaspoons ground cinnamon
2 teaspoons grated orange rind
1 cup (230 g) firmly packed soft
    brown sugar
1/2 cup (45 g) flaked almonds
1/3 cup (35 g) rolled oats
1/2 teaspoon baking powder
1/2 cup (60 g) plain flour
1/3 cup (35 g) soy flour
1/2 teaspoon gluten flour

1 Preheat the oven to moderate 180°C (350°F/Gas 4). Melt 50 g of the soy butter in a saucepan. Add the apple and cook for 10 minutes, or until soft. Add the rhubarb, cinnamon, orange rind and 170 g of the brown sugar and cook gently for a further 2–3 minutes, or until the rhubarb softens. Spoon the mixture into a 15 x 24 cm ovenproof ceramic dish.

2 Combine the almonds, oats, baking powder and remaining brown sugar in a bowl. Sift the flours into a separate bowl. Chop the remaining soy butter and add to the flours. Rub the butter into the flour with your fingertips until crumbly. Stir in the almond mixture and spoon evenly over the rhubarb and apple. Bake for 20–25 minutes, or until lightly golden and brown. Serve hot or warm with the soy custard or soy ice cream.

PEACH CRUMBLE

SOY BAVAROIS WITH MIXED BERRIES

SERVES 4

Dariole moulds are metal moulds used for baked and steamed puddings, or moulding-set puddings and jellies, and give the bavarois its well-known shape. They are available from speciality stores.

Preparation time: 20 minutes +
    4 hours refrigeration
Total cooking time: 10 minutes

soy bean oil, for greasing
2 egg yolks
1/4 cup (60 g) caster sugar
3/4 cup (185 ml) creamy soy milk
1 1/3 gelatine leaves
200 g berry tofu dessert,
    lightly beaten
250 g mixed fresh or frozen berries
    (blackberries, strawberries,
    raspberries, blueberries)
1 tablespoon caster sugar, extra

1　Lightly grease four 100 ml dariole moulds. Combine the egg yolks and sugar in a heatproof bowl. Heat the soy milk in a small saucepan over medium heat until almost boiling. Gradually pour onto the egg mixture, stirring constantly as you pour. Place the bowl over a saucepan of simmering water, ensuring the bottom of the bowl doesn't touch the water, and stir for 10 minutes, or until it thickens and coats the back of a spoon.

2　Soak the gelatine in cold water for 1 minute, or until softened. Squeeze any excess water from the gelatine. Add the gelatine to the egg mixture and stir until dissolved. Place the bowl over iced water to chill, and whisk frequently. When cool, gently whisk in the tofu dessert until thoroughly combined. Pour into the prepared moulds and refrigerate for at least 4 hours, or until set.

3　Place the mixed berries in a saucepan with the extra sugar. Cook, stirring, over low heat for 3–5 minutes, or until the sugar has dissolved. Cool completely.

4　To serve, dip the dariole moulds in hot water for 3–5 seconds and turn out onto serving plates. Spoon the mixed berries and syrup around the bavarois and serve.

APPLE PIE WITH CINNAMON SOY PASTRY

SERVES 4–6

Ground cinnamon is often used for flavouring when mixed in with other ingredients like pastries, cakes and custards. Cinnamon also complements fresh ingredients such as apples, pears and bananas.

Preparation time: 30 minutes + refrigeration
Total cooking time: 45 minutes

1 cup (125 g) plain flour
1 cup (125 g) self-raising flour
1/3 cup (35 g) soy flour
75 g cold butter, chopped
75 g cold soy butter
1/4 cup (60 g) caster sugar
1 teaspoon ground cinnamon

1 egg
1 tablespoon caster sugar, extra

FILLING
2 x 425 g cans pie apples
2 tablespoons caster sugar
1 tablespoon marmalade

1 Sift the flours into a bowl. Rub in the butter and soy butter with your fingertips until the mixture resembles fine breadcrumbs. Add the sugar and cinnamon. Make a well in the centre and stir in the egg and enough water to make a soft dough. Turn out onto a lightly floured surface and knead for 1 minute, or until smooth. Gather together into a ball and wrap in plastic wrap. Refrigerate for at least 1 hour.

2 To make the filling, place the apples, sugar and marmalade in a bowl and mix together well.

3 Divide the dough in half, making one portion a little larger than the other. Roll the larger piece of dough between two sheets of baking paper to fit a 25 cm pie dish. Fit the pastry into the pie dish and trim the edges. The pastry will be soft and it may be necessary to patch as you go.

4 Spread the filling evenly over the pastry base. Roll the remaining pastry between two sheets of baking paper and fit over the top of the apple filling. Trim off any excess pastry, then flute the edges. Make 2–3 small slashes in the pastry as steam vents. Decorate with pastry leaves, using any leftover pastry, if desired. Sprinkle the top with the extra sugar and refrigerate for 20 minutes.

5 Preheat the oven to moderately hot 200°C (400°F/Gas 6). Place a baking tray on the oven shelf. Put the pie dish on the hot tray and bake for 20 minutes. Reduce the heat to moderate 180°C (350°F/Gas 4) and bake for a further 20–25 minutes, or until the pastry is crisp and cooked. To prevent the edges from browning too much, cover with a large sheet of foil that has an 18 cm hole cut out of the centre. Serve the pie hot with soy custard or ice cream.

BLUEBERRY CHEESECAKE

SERVES 6–8

Fresh blueberries are best for this recipe, but are not always available. If they're not in season, use 400 g canned well-drained blueberries or 300 g frozen blueberries, thawed.

Preparation time: 20 minutes +
    2 hours chilling
Total cooking time: 10 minutes

250 g wholemeal biscuits
3 teaspoons ground cinnamon
150 g soy spread or margarine,
    melted
1½ tablespoons gelatine
250 g silken firm tofu
¼ cup (60 g) caster sugar
250 g cream cheese
300 g vanilla soy yoghurt
300 g blueberries

1 Preheat the oven to moderate 180°C (350°F/Gas 4). Grease a 23 cm springform tin.

2 Place the biscuits and 1 teaspoon of the ground cinnamon in a food processor and blend together until it forms fine crumbs. Transfer to a bowl, add the melted soy spread and mix well. Press the crumb mixture onto the base of the prepared tin. Bake for 10 minutes, then cool.

3 Pour ⅔ cup (170 ml) water into a heatproof bowl, evenly sprinkle on the gelatine and leave until spongy—do not stir. Bring a saucepan of water to the boil and remove from the heat. Place the bowl of gelatine in the pan and stir until the gelatine is smooth.

4 Combine the tofu, sugar, cream cheese and yoghurt in a food processor until smooth. Add the gelatine and process in short bursts for 1–2 seconds.

5 Place the blueberries on the biscuit base and pour the tofu mixture over the top, spreading evenly. Chill for at least 2 hours.

6 Remove the side of the tin and dust the cheesecake with the remaining ground cinnamon just before serving.

SOY AT TEATIME

It happens around 3 o'clock in the afternoon. That magic hour when, no matter where you are—at work, at home, out shopping— a voice inside beckons "Time for tea!". Whether your beverage of preference is tea or coffee, it must be accompanied by a little sweet something. This chapter tempts you with favourites such as Pecan and Cinnamon Rolls, Soy Scones and, of course, Chocolate Soy Cake.

PECAN AND CINNAMON ROLLS

MAKES 14

These rolls are an ideal 'sweet something' to have on hand when friends or relatives unexpectedly pop around for a cup of tea or coffee.

Preparation time: 35 minutes +
   1 hour 50 minutes rising
Total cooking time: 25 minutes

1 cup (250 ml) creamy soy milk
2 x 7 g sachets dried yeast
3 cups (375 g) plain flour
1 cup (120 g) soy flour
2 tablespoons gluten flour
1 tablespoon sugar
1/4 teaspoon soy bean oil
1/3 cup (75 g) firmly packed soft
   brown sugar
2 teaspoons ground cinnamon
1 tablespoon soy spread, melted

1/2 cup (60 g) chopped pecans
1/2 cup (60 g) raisins

MAPLE GLAZE
11/2 tablespoons butter
3/4 cup (90 g) sifted icing sugar
11/2 tablespoons maple syrup
1 tablespoon milk

1 Warm 1/2 cup (125 ml) of the soy milk and 1/2 cup (125 ml) water in a small saucepan—do not boil. Transfer to a small bowl. Sprinkle the yeast over the surface and dissolve in the liquid. Leave in a warm place for 10 minutes, or until foamy. If your yeast doesn't foam it is dead and you will have to start again.

2 Combine the flours, sugar and 1 teaspoon salt in a large bowl and make a well in the centre. Add the yeast mixture and the remaining soy milk and mix until well combined. Turn out onto a lightly floured surface and knead for 1 minute, or until the dough forms a smooth ball—add a little extra plain flour if necessary. Grease a large clean bowl with oil, add the dough and turn to coat. Cover with a damp tea towel and leave to rise in a warm place for 1 hour, or until doubled. Combine the brown sugar and cinnamon in a small bowl. Grease two baking trays with soy spread.

3 Turn the dough out onto a lightly floured surface and divide in half. Return one portion to the bowl and cover. Roll out the other to a 24 cm square. Brush the dough with half the melted soy spread, then sprinkle on half the cinnamon sugar mixture, leaving a 1 cm border at the far end. Scatter half the pecans and half the raisins on top. Starting with the edge closest to you, roll up tightly and pinch along the far edge to secure the roll. Repeat with the remaining dough, soy spread and filling ingredients. Cut each roll, seam-side down, into 7 portions (about 3.5 cm wide), then place on the prepared trays, leaving a 3 cm gap between them. Cover with a tea towel and leave in a warm place to rise for 40 minutes. Preheat the oven to moderate 180°C (350°F/Gas 4).

4 Bake for 20 minutes—cover with foil halfway through cooking to prevent over-browning. Cool on a wire rack.

5 To make the maple glaze, melt the butter in a small saucepan over low heat. Remove from the heat and stir in the icing sugar and maple syrup until dissolved, then stir in the milk. Drizzle the glaze over the rolls while still warm.

SOY SCONES

MAKES 10

Tea and scones make up the popular English afternoon snack called 'Devonshire tea', where freshly baked scones are served with strawberry jam and lashings of cream.

Preparation time: 15 minutes
Total cooking time: 12 minutes

1½ cups (185 g) self-raising flour
½ cup (50 g) soy flour
1 teaspoon gluten flour
1 teaspoon baking powder
30 g cold soy butter, chopped
1 tablespoon caster sugar
¾ cup (185 ml) soy milk
soy milk, extra, for brushing

1 Preheat the oven to moderately hot 200°C (400°F/Gas 6). Lightly flour a baking tray. Sift the self-raising, soy and gluten flours and baking powder into a large bowl. Rub the soy butter into the flours with your fingertips until evenly distributed. Stir in the sugar and make a well in the centre.

2 Add almost all the soy milk to the flour mixture and mix lightly with a flat-bladed knife to form a soft dough—add the remaining milk, if needed. Knead briefly on a lightly floured surface until smooth, then pat out to a 2 cm thickness. Cut into rounds with a 4 cm cutter. Place close together on the tray. Gather the remaining dough together and repeat. Brush the top of the scones with the extra soy milk. Bake for 10–12 minutes, or until golden brown. Serve with soy butter and marmalade or jam.

PUMPKIN AND GINGER SOY SCONES

MAKES 20

Although the origins of ginger are unknown, we do know it was one of the first Asian spices to reach south-east Europe. It is said that a baker on the Isle of Rhodes made the first gingerbread around 2400 BC.

Preparation time: 15 minutes
Total cooking time: 12 minutes

1½ cups (240 g) self-raising flour
½ cup (50 g) soy flour
1 teaspoon gluten flour
1 teaspoon baking powder
30 g cold soy butter, chopped
1 tablespoon caster sugar
½ cup (125 g) cooked and mashed
   pumpkin
½ cup (125 ml) soy milk
¼ cup (55 g) glacé ginger
2 tablespoons extra, for brushing

1 Preheat the oven to moderately hot 200°C (400°F/Gas 6). Grease a baking tray. Sift the flours and the baking powder into a large bowl. Rub the soy butter into the flours with your fingertips until evenly distributed. Stir in the sugar and make a well in the centre.

2 Combine the mashed pumpkin, soy milk and a pinch of salt and add almost all of it to the flour mixture. Mix lightly with a flat-bladed knife to form a soft dough—add the remaining liquid, if needed. Finely chop the ginger and stir into the mixture. Gather the dough together and press out onto a lightly floured surface to a 2 cm thickness. Cut into rounds with a 4 cm cutter. Place close together on the tray. Gather the remaining dough together and repeat. Brush the top of the scones with the extra soy milk. Bake for 10–12 minutes, or until golden. Serve with soy butter and honey.

ITALIAN OLIVE LOAF

SERVES 8

This crusty Italian bread is delicious eaten with or without soy butter, as an accompaniment to soup or as a dangerously more-ish snack between meals.

Preparation time: 35 minutes +
   2 hours 25 minutes rising
Total cooking time: 45 minutes

1 teaspoon honey
1 teaspoon dry yeast
3 cups (375 g) plain flour
1/2 cup (50 g) soy flour
1/2 cup (125 ml) tepid soy milk
1/4 cup (35 g) wholemeal flour,
   for dusting
1 1/2 tablespoons fresh thyme,
   chopped
1/2 cup (80 g) pitted Kalamata
   olives, roughly chopped and
   squeezed dry
3 teaspoons soy bean oil
2 tablespoons fine cornmeal,
   for dusting

1 Place the honey and 1/3 cup (80 ml) warm water in a bowl and stir until the honey is dissolved. Sprinkle the yeast over the surface and stir until dissolved. Stand in a warm place for 10 minutes, or until the mixture is foamy. If your yeast doesn't foam, it is dead and you will have to start again.

2 Sift the plain and soy flours and 1 teaspoon salt into a deep bowl and make a well in the centre.

3 Stir the soy milk and 1/2 cup (125 ml) tepid water into the yeast mixture. Pour into the dry ingredients and incorporate the flour and liquid until it forms a ball. Dust a clean surface with the wholemeal flour and turn out the dough. Knead for 8 minutes, or until the dough is smooth and elastic and shaped into a tight ball.

4 Combine the thyme and olives, spread the mixture on the kneading surface, then roll the dough over the top. Gently knead for a further 2 minutes, incorporating the thyme and olives into the dough.

5 Grease a deep, clean bowl with 2 teaspoons of the oil. Add the dough and turn to coat. Cover with a damp tea towel and leave in a warm place for 1 hour 15 minutes, or until doubled in size. Punch down the dough and shape into a round.

6 Grease a round 22 cm cake tin, then dust the base and side with the cornmeal. Place the dough in the prepared cake tin. Brush the surface of the dough with the remaining oil. Cover with a damp tea towel and leave in a warm place for 1 hour, or until doubled in size.

7 Preheat the oven to moderately hot 200°C (400°F/Gas 6). Cut a couple of slashes (2 cm deep and 4 cm long) across the top of the loaf. Bake for 45 minutes, or until the loaf sounds hollow when tapped on the bottom. Cool on a wire cooling rack.

WHOLEMEAL ONION PULL-APART

SERVES 8

This relatively simple idea of alternating portions of dough with cooked onion rings makes for a very impressive addition to any meal, especially soup.

Preparation time: 40 minutes +
   2 hours standing
Total cooking time: 50 minutes

7 g sachet dried yeast
1/2 teaspoon caster sugar
150 g silken tofu, at room
   temperature
1 tablespoon gluten flour
3²/₃ cups (550 g) wholemeal flour
3 tablespoons soy bean oil
2 onions, cut into thin rings

1 Place the yeast, sugar and 1/2 cup (125 ml) warm water in a small bowl. Dissolve the yeast and allow to stand for 8–10 minutes, or until frothy. If your yeast doesn't foam it is dead and you will have to start again. Combine the tofu and 3/4 cup (185 ml) warm water using a fork until smooth.

2 Place the gluten flour, 3¹/₃ cups (500 g) of the wholemeal flour and 1/2 teaspoon salt in a large bowl and make a well in the centre. Add the yeast and tofu mixtures to the dry ingredients, mix with a wooden spoon, then bring the dough together with your hands. Turn out onto a floured surface and knead for 7 minutes, or until smooth and elastic—add the remaining flour, as needed.

3 Grease a large bowl with a little soy oil. Place the dough in the bowl and brush the surface with oil. Cover with a damp tea towel and stand for 1 hour, or until doubled in size.

4 Heat the remaining soy oil in a frying pan. Add the onion and cook over medium heat for 7–8 minutes, or until very soft and golden. Drain on paper towels. Allow to cool.

5 Grease a 9 x 25 cm bread tin and line the base with baking paper. Punch down the dough and knead for a further 2 minutes. Divide the dough into 8 even-size pieces. Form each into 9 cm squarish pieces, flattened slightly to 2 cm thick. Place one square upright against one end of the bread tin, tilt the tin, then spread some of the onion on top. Repeat with the remaining dough and onion, finishing with a square of dough. Cover with a damp tea towel and leave for 45 minutes, or until risen to almost the top of the tin.

6 Preheat the oven to moderately hot 200°C (400°F/Gas 6). Bake for 35–40 minutes, or until golden brown. Leave the bread in the tin for 5 minutes, then turn out onto a wire rack to cool.

SPICED SOY CRACKERS

MAKES 24

These spicy crackers are great dippers for dips such as Soy bean hummus (page 170), Avocado and black bean salsa (page 171) or Soy bean dip (page 172).

Preparation time: 15 minutes +
    1 hour refrigeration
Total cooking time: 20 minutes

1¼ cups (155 g) plain flour
¾ cup (70 g) soy flour
½ teaspoon garam masala
½ teaspoon paprika
2½ tablespoons olive oil
2½ tablespoons lemon juice

1 Place the flours, garam masala, paprika and ½ teaspoon salt in a food processor. Add the oil, lemon juice and 100 ml water and blend until the mixture comes together in a ball. Cover and refrigerate for 1 hour.

2 Preheat the oven to warm 160°C (315°F/Gas 2–3). Line 3 baking trays with baking paper. Cut the dough into 5 or 6 pieces, then roll each piece into rectangles, about 2 mm thick. Cut each piece into long thin triangles (4 cm x 10 cm) and place on the trays. Bake for 20 minutes, or until crisp and lightly coloured. Serve with your favourite dip.

ORANGE AND PISTACHIO BISCOTTI

MAKES 48

There are as many variations of biscotti as there are people who make it. Try replacing the pistachios with pecans, almonds or macadamias, or even adding a little cocoa to the batter.

Preparation time: 15 minutes + cooling
Total cooking time: 45 minutes

2 cups (250 g) self-raising flour
¼ cup (20 g) soy flour
2 teaspoon baking powder
125 g soy butter
1 cup (250 g) sugar
1 tablespoon finely grated orange
    rind
2 eggs
1 teaspoon vanilla essence
¾ cup (100 g) shelled pistachios,
    roughly chopped
2 tablespoons icing sugar

1 Preheat the oven to warm 170°C (325°F/Gas 3). Line 2 baking trays with baking paper. Sift the flours, baking powder and ½ teaspoon salt into a bowl. Beat the soy butter, sugar and rind with electric beaters until creamy. Add the eggs one at a time, beating well after each addition, then beat in the vanilla. Fold in the flour mixture and pistachios with a metal spoon.

2 Divide the dough into 3 portions. Sift the icing sugar onto a worksurface and roll each portion into a 4 cm x 30 cm log. Place the logs on the trays, leaving space between them. Bake for 25 minutes, or until golden. Cool for 10 minutes. Reduce the oven to slow 150°C (300°F/Gas 2). Cut each log into 1.5 cm slices (slightly on the diagonal) with a serrated knife. Place the biscotti on the trays, cut-side down, and bake for a further 15–20 minutes, or until golden and dry.

SPICED SOY CRACKERS

CHOCOLATE CHIP COOKIES

MAKES 16

These cookies look even more enticing if you keep a few chocolate chips aside and pop them on the top of the cookies before baking.

Preparation time: 15 minutes
Total cooking time: 15 minutes

125 g soy butter
1 cup (185 g) soft brown sugar
1 teaspoon vanilla essence
1 egg, lightly beaten
1 tablespoon soy milk
1¼ cups (155 g) plain flour
½ cup (50 g) soy flour
1 teaspoon baking powder
250 g dark chocolate chips

1 Preheat the oven to moderate 180°C (350°F/Gas 4). Line a large baking tray with baking paper.

2 Cream the soy butter and sugar with electric beaters in a large bowl. Mix in the vanilla essence and gradually add the egg, beating well. Stir in the soy milk. Sift the flours and baking powder into a large bowl, then fold into the soy butter and egg mixture. Stir in the choc chips.

3 Drop level tablespoons of the cookie mixture onto the baking tray, leaving about 4 cm between each cookie, then lightly press with a floured fork. Bake for 15 minutes, or until lightly golden. Cool on a wire rack.

WHITE CHOCOLATE AND MACADAMIA COOKIES

MAKES 24

The delicious macadamia is native to Australia, but has been grown in Hawaii since the 1890s. Because it is very difficult to crack it must undergo a strenuous process before it can be shelled.

Preparation time: 15 minutes
Total cooking time: 15 minutes

125 g soy butter
½ cup (125 g) macadamia spread
   (see Note)
200 g firmly packed soft brown sugar
1 egg, lightly beaten
1 teaspoon vanilla essence
1–2 tablespoons soy milk
1½ cups (185 g) plain flour
½ cup (50 g) soy flour
1 teaspoon baking powder
125 g white chocolate chips
125 g macadamia nuts, roughly
   chopped

1 Preheat the oven to moderate 180°C (350°F/Gas 4). Line a baking tray with baking paper. Beat the soy butter, macadamia spread and brown sugar with electric beaters in a large bowl until creamy. Add the egg, vanilla and soy milk and beat well.

2 Sift the flours and baking powder together, then mix into the creamed mixture. Stir in the chocolate chips and macadamias. Drop level tablespoons of mixture onto the tray, leaving about 4 cm between each one. Bake for 12–15 minutes, or until lightly golden. (You may need to bake the cookies in batches depending on the size of your tray.)

Note: Macadamia spread is available from health food stores.

SOY AND LINSEED HERB MUFFINS

MAKES 12

LSA is a mixture made from ground linseed, sunflower seeds and almonds. It is available from the health food section of most supermarkets, or from health food stores.

Preparation time: 15 minutes
Total cooking time: 25 minutes

soy bean oil, for greasing
1½ cups (185 g) self-raising flour
¾ cup (90 g) soy flour
¾ cup (100 g) ground LSA
2 tablespoons chopped fresh chives
2 tablespoons chopped fresh parsley
1 cup (250 ml) soy milk
2 eggs
125 g soy spread, melted and cooled

1 Preheat the oven to moderately hot 200°C (400°F/Gas 6). Lightly grease twelve ½ cup muffin holes.

2 Sift the self-raising and soy flours into a large bowl, then stir in the LSA. Season well. Stir in the herbs, then make a well in the centre. Whisk the milk and eggs together in a jug, add to the dry ingredients with the melted soy spread and gently fold together with a metal spoon. Do not overmix—the batter should be lumpy. Overmixing will produce tough muffins.

3 Fill each muffin hole three-quarters full with the mixture. Bake for 20–25 minutes, or until golden brown and firm to the touch. Allow to cool for a couple of minutes, then gently loosen each muffin with a flat-bladed knife and lift out onto a wire rack. Delicious served warm with soup or with casseroles.

SOY FRUIT MUFFINS

MAKES 6 LARGE MUFFINS

These muffins are filled with naturally sweet dried fruits, a combination sure to please everyone, and are an ideal quick breakfast on the run.

Preparation time: 20 minutes
Total cooking time: 30 minutes

1/2 cup (50 g) soy flour, sifted
3/4 cup (75 g) rye flour, sifted
1/2 cup (80 g) brown rice flour, sifted
3/4 cup (75 g) rolled oats
2 1/2 teaspoons baking powder
1/2 cup (125 g) caster sugar
1 egg
3 tablespoons soy bean oil
1 1/2 cups (375 ml) soy milk
1/2 cup (80 g) chopped dried dates
1/2 cup (60 g) chopped dried bananas
1/3 cup (60 g) chopped dried figs
dried figs, chopped, extra, to garnish

1 Preheat the oven to moderate 180°C (350°F/Gas 4). Lightly grease six 1 cup muffin holes.

2 Place the soy, rye and brown rice flours, oats, baking powder and sugar in a bowl, then make a well in the centre. Whisk the egg, oil and soy milk in a jug and add to the dry ingredients. Add the dried dates, bananas and figs and fold gently with a metal spoon until just combined. Do not overmix—the batter should be lumpy. Overmixing will produce tough muffins.

3 Fill each muffin hole two-thirds full with the mixture. Top with an extra piece of dried fig. Bake for 30 minutes, or until the muffins come away slightly from the sides of the tin. Allow to cool for a couple of minutes, then gently loosen each muffin with a flat-bladed knife and lift out onto a wire rack to cool.

SOY BROWNIES

MAKES 24

Carob is the powdered dried inner pulp of the carob bean and is a handy substitute for chocolate. The pod is also called 'Saint John's Bread' after a theory that Saint John the Baptist subsisted on that, not locusts.

Preparation time: 15 minutes
Total cooking time: 30 minutes

1 cup (125 g) plain flour
1/2 cup (50 g) soy flour
1 teaspoon baking powder
1/3 cup (40 g) carob or cocoa
    powder
1/2 cup (60 g) chopped pecans
125 g butter, chopped
250 g soy chocolate, broken into
    pieces
1 cup (185 g) soft brown sugar
150 g silken firm tofu
2 eggs, lightly beaten
icing sugar, for dusting

1 Preheat the oven to moderate 180°C (350°F/Gas 4). Lightly grease a shallow 20 x 30 cm baking tin and line with enough baking paper to overlap on the longer sides—this will help when removing the brownies from the tin after cooking.

2 Sift the flours, baking powder and carob into a large bowl. Add the pecans and make a well in the centre.

3 Place the butter, soy chocolate and brown sugar in a heatproof bowl. Place over a saucepan of simmering water, stirring frequently until the butter and chocolate have melted and combined. Set aside to cool slightly.

4 Mash the tofu well with a potato masher or fork and add to the dry ingredients. Add the eggs and the melted chocolate mixture and mix well with a metal spoon or a spatula. Pour the mixture into the prepared tin and bake for 25 minutes, or until firm. Cool in the tin. To serve, cut into slices and dust with icing sugar.

COCONUT PINE SLICE

Experiment with different types of nuts or seeds, such as almonds or pumpkin seeds, for another taste sensation while maintaining the texture.

Preparation time: 20 minutes
Total cooking time: 40 minutes

1/3 cup (20 g) shredded coconut
3/4 cup (90 g) self-raising flour
1/2 cup (50 g) soy flour
3/4 cup (140 g) soft brown sugar
2 tablespoons sunflower seeds
2 tablespoons sesame seeds
1/2 cup (70 g) chopped
    macadamias
1/3 cup (55 g) chopped dates
1 tablespoon chopped glacé
    ginger

1/2 cup (45 g) desiccated coconut
3/4 cup (230 g) canned crushed
    pineapple, drained
100 g soy spread or margarine,
    melted
2 eggs, lightly beaten

ICING
2 cups (250 g) icing sugar
30 g soy spread, melted
1 1/2 tablespoons lemon juice

1 Preheat the oven to warm 170°C (325°F/Gas 3). Spread the coconut evenly on a baking tray and toast for 5–8 minutes, or until lightly golden. Grease a 20 x 30 cm shallow baking tin and line with enough baking paper to overlap on the longer sides—this will make the slice easier to remove once baked.

2 Sift the self-raising and soy flours into a large bowl. Add the brown sugar, seeds, macadamias, dates, ginger and desiccated coconut. Stir in the pineapple, melted soy spread and beaten egg and mix well.

3 Spoon the mixture into the prepared tin. Bake for 25–30 minutes, or until golden brown. Cool in the tin, remove and cover with the icing.

4 To make the icing, combine the icing sugar, melted soy spread and lemon juice in a small bowl. Stir in 1–2 teaspoons of boiling water to reach a smooth consistency. Spread evenly over the slice. Sprinkle the top with the toasted shredded coconut and when set, slice and serve.

CITRUS AND YOGHURT CAKE

SERVES 8

The sweet citrus syrup is absorbed into the cake, making it a moist offering suitable as a dessert cake. Serve with a dollop of thick cream.

Preparation time: 25 minutes +
    20 minutes standing
Total cooking time: 1 hour

200 g soy butter
1 cup (250 g) caster sugar
2 teaspoons grated lemon rind
4 eggs, separated
2¼ cups (280 g) plain flour
⅓ cup (35 g) soy flour
1 teaspoon baking powder
1 teaspoon bicarbonate of soda
200 g vanilla soy yoghurt

LEMON SYRUP
2 teaspoons grated lemon rind
1 large strip lemon rind
½ cup (125 ml) lemon juice
¾ cup (185 g) caster sugar
1 fresh lemon leaf, optional

1 Preheat the oven to moderate 180°C (350°F/Gas 4). Lightly grease a 22 cm springform tin and line the base with baking paper. Beat the soy butter, sugar and lemon rind with electric beaters until light and creamy. Add the egg yolks one at a time, beating well after each addition. Transfer to a large bowl.

2 Sift the flours, baking powder and bicarbonate of soda together and fold into the creamed mixture in thirds, alternately with the soy yoghurt.

3 Beat the egg whites with electric beaters until firm (but not stiff) peaks form. Fold a large spoonful of egg white into the cake mixture to soften, then gently fold in the remaining egg white until incorporated.

4 Spoon into the tin and smooth the surface. Bake for 50 minutes, or until a skewer comes out clean when inserted into the centre of the cake. Cover with foil during the last 15 minutes if the surface is browning too much. Leave in the tin and place on a metal tray. Insert small holes all over the surface of the cake with a thin skewer.

5 To make the lemon syrup, combine the lemon rinds and juice, sugar, lemon leaf and ¼ cup (60 ml) water in a small saucepan. Stir over low heat until the sugar is dissolved. Boil without stirring, for 10 minutes, or until thick and syrupy. Remove the lemon strip and lemon leaf and reserve. Pour the hot syrup over the warm cake and leave for 20 minutes to allow the syrup to absorb. Gently remove from the tin and serve with cream. If desired, garnish with the reserved lemon strip and leaf.

CHOCOLATE SOY CAKE

SERVES 8–12

One of the three fruit sugars, fructose has a sweetening power far greater than glucose or sucrose, so don't use it as a substitute for normal sugar.

Preparation time: 30 minutes +
    overnight chilling
Total cooking time: 1 hour 30 minutes

ICING
3/4 cup (160 g) fructose
1/2 cup (60 g) cocoa powder
150 ml soy milk
1 teaspoon vanilla essence

21/4 cups (280 g) plain flour
3/4 cup (90 g) cocoa powder
1/2 teaspoon baking powder
1/2 teaspoon bicarbonate of soda
2 eggs
4 egg whites
2/3 cup (170 ml) soy milk
2 tablespoons instant coffee
    dissolved in 3 tablespoons
    hot water
1 teaspoon vanilla essence
240 g soy spread
3 cups (645 g) fructose
icing sugar, for dusting

1 To make the icing, combine the fructose and cocoa powder in a saucepan. Whisk in half the soy milk to form a smooth paste, then add the remaining soy milk. Bring to the boil over medium heat, then reduce the heat and simmer for 3 minutes—stir constantly with a wooden spoon. Remove from the heat and stir in the essence. Pour through a fine sieve and chill overnight.

2 Preheat the oven to moderate 180°C (350°F/Gas 4). Lightly grease a 3 litre bundt tin.

3 Sift the plain flour, cocoa, baking powder, bicarbonate of soda and 1/2 teaspoon salt into a large bowl. In a separate bowl, whisk the whole eggs and the egg whites until well mixed. Combine the soy milk, coffee and vanilla essence.

4 Cream the soy spread in a bowl using electric beaters, then gradually add the fructose. Beat on high speed for 2 minutes. Gradually add the egg mixture and beat for 3 minutes. Reduce the speed to low and add one third of the dry ingredients, scraping down the sides. Increase to medium speed and beat in half the soy milk mixture. Beat in the remaining dry ingredients alternately with the soy milk mixture until combined. Spoon into the prepared tin.

5 Bake for 1 hour 15 minutes to 1 hour 30 minutes, or until a skewer comes out clean when inserted into the centre of the cake. Cover the cake with foil halfway through if the surface begins to overbrown. Leave to cool in the tin. Turn out on a serving platter, dust with icing sugar and drizzle with the icing.

COOKERY TERMS

AL DENTE

An Italian phrase meaning 'to the tooth', usually used to describe pasta. Means slightly underdone, so the pasta (and sometimes vegetables) are cooked to a point where there is still some 'bite'.

BAIN-MARIE

Also called a 'water bath'. A baking dish is half-filled with water so delicate food (in its own cooking vessel) is protected from direct heat. Often used when baking custards.

BAKE BLIND

To bake an empty pastry case before the filling is added. This ensures the pastry is cooked through and not soggy. The pastry is usually lined with baking paper and filled with baking beads or uncooked rice or beans so it keeps its shape while cooking.

BASTE

To spoon or brush cooking juices or other fat over food during cooking to prevent drying out or help with heat transfer.

BOUQUET GARNI

A small bunch of herbs (commonly thyme, bay leaf and parsley) tied in a bundle, or wrapped in muslin, which is used to flavour stocks, soups and stews. Remove the bundle before serving. Other variations may include celery leaves and peppercorns.

BROWN

To pan-fry, bake, grill or roast food (such as meat) so the outer surface turns a golden brown colour—this is due to caramelisation.

CREAM

To beat butter or butter and sugar together until light and creamy.

CUBE

To chop food into even cubes. Usually bite-sized for use in soups or stews.

DICE

To chop food into very small, even cubes.

ESCALOPE

Very thin slice of meat cut from a large muscle without the bone, gristle or sinew, often from the top of the leg or the fillet, which is beaten out until very thin prior to frying. Often veal or chicken.

FILLET

To cut the meat, fish or poultry away from the bone. It also refers to the particular cut of meat (eg pork or lamb), commonly taken from the top half of an animal's leg.

FOLD

To mix one ingredient into another very gently (usually flour or egg whites) with a metal spoon or plastic spatula. The idea is to combine the mixture without losing the air. To fold properly, cut through the centre of the mixture, then run the edge of the spoon or spatula around the outer edge of the bowl, turning the bowl as you go.

GLAZE

A substance (often warmed jam or beaten egg) brushed over food to give it shine and colour.

GREASE

To lightly coat a tin or dish with oil or melted butter to prevent food sticking.

INFUSE

To flavour a liquid by heating it with aromatic ingredients (such as a vanilla bean or cinnamon stick) and leaving to let the flavour develop.

JULIENNE

To cut into uniform thin matchsticks for quick cooking. Often used for stir-fries or in French cuisine.

KNEAD

To stretch and fold dough to make it firm and smooth. This stretches the gluten in the flour and gives elasticity. Used for bread making but not for pastry making (over-handling will make pastry tough).

MARINATE

To tenderise and flavour food (usually meat) by leaving it in an acidulated seasoned liquid (a marinade).

PARBOIL

To partially cook in boiling water before some other form of cooking. Most commonly used for roast potatoes, which are parboiled before being added to the roasting tin.

PINCH

A small amount of something—as much as can be held between your thumb and forefinger.

POACH

To cook food immersed in a gently simmering liquid.

PUNCH DOWN THE DOUGH

A term used in bread making. A yeast dough that is left to rise is then punched with one firm blow of the fist, to remove the air from it.

PUREE

Food blended or processed to a pulp.

REDUCE

To boil or simmer liquid in an uncovered pan so that the liquid evaporates and the mixture becomes thicker and more concentrated in flavour. Most soups and stews are reduced—this should usually be done at a simmer so the flavour of the dish is not impaired by long, hard boiling.

RIND

The coloured skin of citrus fruits (avoid the bitter white pith), more commonly lemon, orange and lime. Often grated and added to mixtures.

ROUX

The base of many sauces—a basic mixture of fat (usually melted butter) and flour cooked over low heat. The roux acts as a thickener for the sauce once liquid (usually milk) is gradually added. The most common of these roux-based sauces is a béchamel sauce.

RUB IN

To mix together flour and butter with your fingertips until the mixture resembles fine breadcrumbs. Usually used when making pastry.

SCORE

To ensure even cooking, make incisions with a knife (usually into fish or meat) in a criss-cross pattern, without cutting all the way through.

SIFT

To shake dry ingredients (usually flour) through a sieve to aerate and remove lumps.

SIMMER

To cook liquid, or food in liquid, over low heat, below boiling point. The surface of the liquid will be moving with a few small bubbles.

SKIM

To remove fat or scum that comes to the surface of a liquid.

SOFT PEAKS

A term used when egg whites are whipped. The peak will fold over on itself when the beater is lifted.

STIFF PEAKS

A term used when egg whites are whipped. The peak will hold its shape when the beater is lifted.

STRAIN

To remove solids from a liquid by pouring through a sieve. The solids are discarded, unless specified.

WHISK

To beat rapidly with a wire whisk, to incorporate air and add volume.

INDEX

A

Amaretto syrup, Coffee soy ice cream with, 187
Apple and rhubarb crumble, 196
apple, Barley with caramelised, 38
Apple pie with cinnamon soy pastry, 200
Asian greens and shiitake mushrooms, Tofu with, 90
Avocado and black bean salsa, 173
avocado aïoli, Beer-battered tempeh with wedges and, 101

B

Baked custards with poached tamorillos, 188
Banana bread, 37
banana breakfast, Maple, 51
banana terrine, Frozen mango and, 180
Barley with caramelised apple, 38
bean curd (see tofu)
bean curd sheets, 16
Bean curd sushi, 171
beef
    Chinese beef in soy, 148
    Ma po tofu with beef mince, 160
    Teriyaki beef stir-fry with soy beans, 164
Beer-battered tempeh with wedges and avocado aïoli, 101
berries, Soy bavarois with mixed, 199
Bircher muesli, 34
biscotti, Orange and pistachio, 214
black beans, 16
    Avocado and black bean salsa, 173
    Black bean pancakes with bok choy, 125
    Tofu in black bean sauce, 105
Blueberry cheesecake, 203
bok choy, Black bean and coriander pancakes with, 125
Boston baked soy beans, 132
Bread and butter pudding, 191
brownies, Soy, 222

burgers
    Soy and mushroom burgers, 57
    Soy lentil burgers with peanut sauce, 70

C

cakes
    Chocolate soy cake, 229
    Citrus and yoghurt cake, 226
Caramel rice pudding, 179
carbonara, Soy pasta, 140
Carob peanut smoothie, 50
Carrot and leek tart, 54
Cauliflower cheese, 87
celeriac, Tofu, and potato rösti, 42
cheesecake
    Blueberry cheesecake, 203
    Chocolate tofu cheesecake, 195
cheese (soy), 20
    Cauliflower cheese, 87
    Macaroni cheese, 122
chicken
    Five-spice soy chicken, 86
    Miso yakitori chicken, 136
    Miso yakitori chicken balls, 136
    Phad Thai with tofu, chicken and prawns, 156
    Teriyaki chicken and soy bean stir-fry, 164
chilli bean paste, 16
Chilli con carne with soy beans, 143
chilli jam, Peanut and lime-crusted tofu with, 109
Chinese beef in soy, 148
Chinese hot and sour soup, 69
Chinese-style steamed fish, 135
chocolate
    Chocolate chip cookies, 217
    Chocolate mousse, 176
    Chocolate soy cake, 229
    Chocolate tofu cheesecake, 195
    Soy brownies, 222
    White chocolate and macadamia cookies, 217
cinnamon soy pastry, Apple pie with, 200

ACKNOWLEDGEMENTS

Recipe Development: Judy Clarke, Michelle Earl, Vicky Harris, Katy Holder, Jane Lawson, Valli Little, Nadine McCristal, Kerrie Mullins, Kate Murdoch, Sally Parker, Tracy Rutherford, Claudio Sherbini, Melita Smilovic.
Home Economists: Alison Adams, Ross Dobson, Sonia Greig, Justine Johnson, Kim Passenger, Anna Phillips, Angela Tregonning, Wendy Quisumbing.

This edition published in the United States and Canada by Whitecap Books.
Published by Murdoch Books® a division of Murdoch Magazines Pty Ltd,
GPO Box 1203, Sydney NSW Australia 1045
Phone: (612) 4352 7000   Fax: (612) 4352 7026

Managing Editor: Rachel Carter. Editor: Stephanie Kistner.
Creative Director: Marylouise Brammer. Concept and design: Michelle Cutler.
Food Director: Jane Lawson. Food Editors: Vanessa Broadfoot, Melita Smilovic.
Photographer: Rob Reichenfeld. Stylist: Cherise Koch. Food Preparation: Valli Little.

Chief Executive: Mark Smith
Publisher: Kay Scarlett
Production Manager: Liz Fitzgerald

ISBN 1 55285 228 8

Printed by Toppan Printing Co. (Hong Kong) Ltd.
PRINTED IN CHINA

Whitecap Books Ltd (Vancouver Office)
351 Lynn Avenue, North Vancouver, BC
Canada V7J 2C4

Whitecap Books Ltd (Toronto Office)
47 Coldwater Road, North York, ON
Canada M3B IY8

Graphic Arts Center Publishing
P.O. Box 10306, Portland, OR
USA 97296-0306